Tales of Mystery and the Unknown

THE GLOBE READER'S COLLECTION

TALES OF MYSTERY AND THE UNKNOWN

ROBERT R. POTTER

GLOBE BOOK COMPANY
A Division of Simon & Schuster
Englewood Cliffs, New Jersey

Dr. Potter is author of Globe's *Myths and Folktales Around the World, Stories Beyond Time and Space, Stories of Surprise and Wonder, English Everywhere, Making Sense, Writing a Research Paper,* and *Language Workshop.* He is the consulting editor of *American Folklore and Legends* and the *Pathways to the World of English* series.

Cover Art: *House by the Railroad,* 1925, Edward Hopper. Oil on canvas, 24" × 29". The Museum of Modern Art, New York. Given anonymously.
Cover Design: Marek Antoniak

ISBN: 0-83590-162-9

Printed in the United States of America.
10 9

Globe Book Company
A Division of Simon & Schuster
Englewood Cliffs, New Jersey

Acknowledgments

We thank the following authors and companies for their permission to use copyrighted material:

COLLINS-KNOWLTON-WING, INC.—for "Starbride" by Anthony Boucher. Copyright © 1951 by Anthony Boucher. Adapted and reprinted by permission of Collins-Knowlton-Wing.

J M DENT & SONS LTD—for Canadian rights to "August Heat" by W.F. Harvey. Adapted with permission.

E.P. DUTTON & CO., INC.—For "August Heat" from *The Beast With Five Fingers* by William Fryer Harvey. Copyright 1947 by E.P. Dutton & Co., Inc., and adapted and reprinted with their permission.

ANN ELMO AGENCY, INC.—For "Man With a Problem" by Donald Honig. Copyright, 1958, by Donald Honig. Adapted with permission.

HART PUBLISHING COMPANY, INC.—for "The Devil in Devonshire" from *This Baffling World* by John Godwin, copyright 1968 Hart Publishing Company, Inc. Adapted with permission.

HAROLD MATSON COMPANY, INC.—for "The Chaser" by John Collier, copyright 1940, 1969 by John Collier, adapted and reprinted by permission of Harold Matson Co., Inc.;—for "The Holiday Man" by Richard Matheson, copyright © 1957 by Richard Matheson, adapted and reprinted by permission of Harold Matson Co., Inc.

DAVID McKAY CO., INC.—for "The Canvas Bag" by Alan E. Nourse, adapted by permission of the author and David McKay Company, Inc., New York, N.Y., from *The Counterfeit Man: More Science Fiction Stories* by Alan E. Nourse. Copyright © 1953, 1954, 1955, 1956, 1963 by Alan E. Nourse.

PARKER PUBLISHING CO., INC.—for a selection from the book *The Enigma of the Poltergeist* by Raymond Bayless © 1967 by Parker Publishing Co., Inc. Published by Parker Publishing Company, Inc., West Nyack, New York. Adapted with permission.

POPULAR PUBLICATIONS, INC.—for "Letter to the Editor" by Morris Hershman. Copyright 1953 by Popular Publications. Adapted with permission.

LYLE STUART, INC.—for "The Girl Who Lived Twice" from *Stranger Than Science Fiction* by Frank Edwards. Adapted with permission.

Contents

Exploring the Unknown

A Science Fiction Sampler

Strange . . . and True?

A Warning, A Promise

The spine-tingling tales in this book are not for everybody. They take place in an unreal world where anything can happen. If you like your world to be neat and normal, don't read these stories on an empty stomach or after your family has gone to bed. Demons don't mix well with dreams.

As you may have noticed, the book has three sections. The first, "Exploring the Unknown," offers eight strange stories. They come from around the world. Some were written years ago, others only recently. In each of them, the only thing we can count on is the unexpected. Surprises lie waiting on nearly every page.

"A Science Fiction Sampler," the second section, contains six samples of a kind of literature that may be new to you. The author of a science fiction story usually pretends that something now impossible has suddenly been made possible. Then things start jumping in a brand new world of the imagination. You don't have to like science to love science fiction. Wait and see.

The last section is called "Strange . . . and True?" It will tease your mind with reports of "supernatural" events that are supposed to have really happened. No one will force you to believe that these things are true, but you may have to force yourself *not* to believe some of them. It's up to you.

Taken in small doses, *Tales of Mystery and the Unknown* is good mental medicine. Its strange stories will hold your attention. The questions on each story will help you to check your understanding and to think about important subjects in a new way. As you'll discover, a really good surprise story does more than chill the blood; it also provides tempting food for serious thought.

Ready to go? All right, just turn the page with this promise in mind: *You'll remember some of the stories in this book as long as you live.* If you don't, you've got antifreeze in your blood vessels. And *that's* really strange!

Man with a Problem

Donald Honig

Just imagine . . . *You're walking down the busy main street of a big city. It's a beautiful sunny day. Suddenly you notice that everyone around you is looking up. You look up too—twenty-six stories up—and see a man on a window ledge. What would you do? Some people around you might be shouting: "Come on, Chicken, let's go!" "Afraid to take a little dive?" "I ain't got all day, Buddy." Others might be praying, silently or aloud. Again, what would* you *do? You might ask yourself, "Who is this man?" "What's he done that he wants to take his own life?" "How could anyone get in such a mess?" To you, the answers to these questions would be unknown, but there'd be no doubt that he was a "Man with a Problem."*

Vocabulary Preview

BELLHOP (BEL-hop) hotel worker who carries suitcases to the rooms of guests.

• A *bellhop* showed the woman to her hotel room.

CANVAS (KAN-vus) very heavy cloth

• The tent was made of strong *canvas.*

CLERGYMAN (KLUR-jee-mun) a religious leader; a minister, priest, or rabbi

• A *clergyman* started the graduation services with a prayer.

INHALED (in-HAYLD) breathed in; drew into the lungs

• The smoke *inhaled* by cigarette smokers can cause cancer.

LEDGE (LEJ) a narrow flat place on a mountain or building

• The mountain climbers stopped on a *ledge* to rest.

THE MAN STOOD QUIETLY ON A NARROW ledge outside the hotel. He watched the people gathering far below on the sidewalk. The crowd had become a sea of curious white and black faces. It was growing fast, swelling out into the street. New people joined the crowd like hurrying bugs, drawn into the rest as if by something to eat. The traffic was beginning to back up. Horns sounded loudly. It all looked very tiny and mysterious from twenty-six stories up. The sounds that reached him were faint, but the excitement in them was all too clear.

He was paying little attention to the surprised faces that kept popping in and out of the window to look or to talk. First it had been a bellhop, staring and shaking his head; then an elevator operator who in a hard voice had demanded to know what this was all about.

He looked at the elevator operator's face. "What do you think it is all about?" he asked in a quiet voice.

"You gonna jump?" the elevator operator asked.

"Go away," the man on the ledge said. He looked again down at the street.

"You won't walk away from a jump like that," the elevator operator growled, as his head disappeared.

A moment later another head poked through the window. The man on the ledge didn't know who it was.

"I beg your pardon," the head said.

The man waved him away.

"You're thinking of a very foolish thing," the head declared.

The man paid no attention.

The hotel manager finally appeared, a fat red face that

first looked down and then looked over at the man standing on the ledge.

"What are you doing out there?" the manager asked.

"I'm going to jump."

"Who are you? What's your name?"

"Carl Adams. And the reason why I'm doing this does not concern you."

"Think what you're doing, man," the manager said, his fat chin shaking as he spoke, his face turning even redder.

"I've thought about it. Now go away and leave me alone."

The ledge was narrow, about eighteen inches wide. He stood between two windows, but there was no chance of reaching him from either of the windows. His back was against the wall, the bright sun falling full upon him. He had left his jacket inside. His shirt was open at the throat.

More heads kept poking through the window. They spoke quietly to him, calling him "Mr. Adams." Some spoke to him with pity, as though they knew somehow that the man was completely insane. Each told the man who he was: a doctor, a hotel official, a clergyman.

"Why not come in and talk it over?" the clergyman asked gently.

"There's nothing left to say," Adams said.

"Do you want me to come out and guide you back through the window?"

"If you or anyone else steps out," Adams said, "so help me, I'll jump."

"Can't you tell us your problem?"

"No."

"How can we help you then?"

"You can't. Go away."

For a while no one came to the window. And then a

policeman's head popped out, looking at him for a moment with an odd smile.

"Hey, fella," the policeman said.

Adams looked at him, studying his face. "What do you want?" he asked.

"They called me up from traffic duty downstairs. Said there's a guy up here threatening to take a dive. You're not really going to jump, are you?"

"Yes."

"What do you want to do that for?"

"It's my nature to do funny things."

"Hey, you got a real sense of humor," the policeman said. He pushed his cap back on his head, sitting out on the window sill. "I like that. Want a cigarette?"

"No," Adams said.

The policeman shook a cigarette loose from his pack and lighted it. He inhaled deeply, blowing the smoke out into the sunshine where the wind snapped it up. "It's sure a pretty day, you know?"

"A good day to die," Adams said, looking at him.

"You're in a sad way, fella. You got a family?"

"No. Do you?"

"I've got a wife."

"Well, I have no one."

"That's too bad."

"Yes," Adams said. It wasn't so long ago that I did have a family, he thought. Only yesterday in fact. He had left the house in the morning to go to work and Karen had said good-by to him at the door (not kissed him, as she used to do; theirs was a kissless marriage now, but she was still his wife, he still loved only her, then and forever, would never give her the divorce, remained firm about that even though she said she would leave him some time). And then he had come home at six o'clock and there was no wife any more, no love, nothing, only the empty bottle of sleeping pills—suicide pills—and the note and the silent apartment . . . and Karen's body lying on the couch.

She had left the note on his pillow. It was written neatly, thoughtfully, explaining. Steve had told her he could not go away with her. Steve had fooled her. (The note was that open, that honest; she could mention Steve like that and he would know—as he had known for months now. Once he had even seen them together in a neighborhood bar. There had been nothing dishonest about it on her part. She told him then that their marriage was over, spoke freely of Steve to him.)

He had gone out that night and walked the streets until after midnight, come back to the house and gone to sleep. He awoke that morning knowing that his mind had been made up, that he was going to do this which he was now planning. He walked to this part of town and got a room in the hotel, asking for a room near the top. He knew that what would happen after that would happen naturally, as something that was supposed, somehow, to happen.

The streets were crowded with curious people now. The police had forced the crowd back, making a great clear place directly below, should he decide to jump. He could see the firemen standing with their canvas life-net that looked like a round black pancake, a red circle painted in the center. But he knew that the canvas pancake could do nothing for a body dropping twenty-six floors. There was no way the people below could save him. The fire ladders did not reach that high.

"This is useless, senseless," a man was saying to him, his head leaning out of the window.

"You might think so," Adams said.

"Look, I'm a doctor," the man said. "I can help you."

"You think I'm a nut?"

"No, Mr. Adams. But I can help you."

"It's too late now."

"If you jump then it will be too late. Now there's still time."

"You'd better go and help somebody who needs you, doctor. I don't need you."

The doctor disappeared. Adams stared once more down at the crowds. Already he felt the strange nearness of death separating him from other men. He was different now, apart and alone. All those people down there waiting, waiting. They'll see something all right, he thought. And those men in the room, he could hear them talking, always talking, figuring ways of talking to him.

He looked around; a face was out the window, staring at him. It was the clergyman again, a round, interested, honest face.

"Is there anything we can do for you?" the clergyman asked.

"No," he said.

"Do you want to come in now?"

"You're wasting your time, father."

"I'm not wasting my time."

"Yes, you are. I'm not coming in."

"Do you want us to leave you alone to think?"

"Do as you please."

The clergyman's head disappeared. He was alone again. He watched the crowds, a soft joy in his eyes now. The height did not bother him any longer, as it had when he had first stepped out onto the ledge.

He wondered what the men in the room were planning. Ropes? Ladders? Nets? Chairs hanging from the roof? They would have to be very careful, he knew, because they were never quite sure what his state of mind was.

The policeman appeared again. Adams knew he would. Adams had talked more to the policeman than to any of the others, and so the policeman would try again.

"You know, Adams," the officer said, sitting out on the window sill, "in a way, you're doing me a favor."

"How's that?"

"Well, usually I'd be down there taking care of traffic. But because of you I'm up here taking it easy."

"Is that so?"

"That's so."

"You might just as well be up here. That traffic isn't moving anyway."

The policeman laughed. "That's right," he said. "Those people down there," he said, pointing, "are expecting you to jump. They're looking forward to it."

Adams looked at him. "Looking forward to it?"

"Sure. They've made up their minds that you're going to jump and they want to see it. You going to disappoint them?"

Adams looked down, his eyes sweeping over the blocks and blocks of crowded people.

"You can't hear them up here," the policeman said, "but they're yelling for you to jump."

"Are they?"

"Uh-huh. They feel you owe them that for making them stand around here all afternoon."

"They're like a pack of hungry wolves," Adams said.

"That's right. Why give up your life just so they can have a thrill?" The policeman watched Adams' face closely. "Come on in," he said in a low, friendly voice. "The hell with all those people."

"Maybe you're right," Adams said.

"Sure."

Adams leaned forward, his back coming away from the wall for a moment. Then he fell back, covering his eyes for a second.

"What's the matter?" the policeman asked.

"I guess I'm a bit dizzy. Maybe you'd better give me a hand."

The policeman looked at the rooftops across the street. Photographers from the newspapers were waiting to take pictures there. It would make quite a picture for the morning papers.

"All right," the policeman said. "Hold on."

The crowd sent up a roar of thrill and terror when they saw the policeman climb out of the window and stand on the ledge, just a few feet from the man in the white shirt. They watched the policeman move slowly along the ledge, carefully holding out his hand.

Adams reached his hand toward the policeman's.

"I knew you would come up some time," Adams said. "That's why I chose this place."

"What?" the policeman said, trying to keep his balance on the narrow ledge. "What do you mean?"

"My name isn't Adams, Steve. Karen was my wife. Do you know that last night she . . . ."

White terror spread over the policeman's face as he tried to draw back, but his hand was locked in the other man's, and then there was a sudden pull and sickening twist as he began to fall softly out into space, toward the rising roar from the crowd. The last thing he felt was the firm, hard hand gripping his like an iron claw.

Recall

1. At first "Adams" gave the faces at the window (a) no attention (b) little attention (c) a great deal of attention.

2. "Adams" wasn't worried that the canvas "pancake" might save him because (a) he could easily jump to the left or right of it (b) he knew he really wasn't going to jump (c) he knew he would be falling too far and too fast for the pancake to save him.
3. Among the people at the window was a (a) relative (b) doctor (c) man with a rope.
4. When he first spoke to "Adams," the police officer said he (a) had been called up from the street below (b) was a specialist in suicide cases (c) knew who "Adams" really was.
5. The person who tried most to joke with "Adams" was the (a) bellhop (b) elevator operator (c) police officer.
6. Karen was (a) Steve's sister (b) Steve's wife (c) "Adams'" wife.
7. While standing on the ledge, "Adams" spent some time thinking about (a) his money (b) Karen (c) his childhood.
8. According to the police officer, people in the crowd were (a) making almost no noise (b) yelling for "Adams" to jump (c) praying he would not jump.
9. "They're like a pack of hungry wolves," Adams said. *They* refers to (a) the people in the room (b) the news photographers (c) the crowd below.
10. The person who finally learned about "Adams'" problem was the (a) police officer (b) clergyman (c) doctor.

Infer

11. "Adams" had chosen to stand on a ledge of that particular hotel because (a) Steve was on traffic duty nearby (b) it was in the right spot to draw a big crowd (c) he hated the hotel manager.

12. When "Adams" stepped out onto the ledge, he (a) had no definite plan (b) had a definite plan to jump (c) was probably too excited and upset to think.

13. At the beginning of the story, "Adams" had probably been on the ledge (a) a few minutes (b) many hours (c) a day or so.

14. "Adams" used this false name because he (a) wanted to die unknown (b) was too disturbed to remember his real name (c) didn't want Steve to know who he really was.

15. When he first spoke to the police officer, "Adams" talked more to him than to the others because (a) he really liked the police officer (b) he had no use for clergymen (c) he wanted the police officer to come back to the window again later.

16. One of the reasons the police officer stepped out on the ledge was probably that (a) the clergyman asked him to (b) the mayor was watching (c) news photographers were taking pictures.

17. Which of the following groups of words refer to the same person? (a) Karen's lover; "Adams"; the hotel manager (b) the police officer; "Adams"; Karen's lover (c) Karen's lover; Steve; the police officer.

18. The story contains little (a) conversation (b) excitement (c) description of main characters.

19. At the end of the story, when "Adams" said he was dizzy and asked for Steve's hand, he was probably (a) telling the truth (b) lying (c) trying to help Steve.

20. During the course of the story there were (a) two suicides and two murders (b) one suicide and two murders (c) two suicides and one murder.

Vocabulary Review

1. The fire fighter *inhaled* too much smoke. *Inhaled* means (a) saw (b) drove through (c) breathed.
2. Maury works as a *bellhop.* Maury works in a (a) church (b) hotel (c) fire department.
3. Three *clergymen* spoke at the meeting. A *clergyman* is a (a) religious leader (b) cleaning expert (c) nearly insane person.
4. The explorers spent the night on a rocky *ledge.* A *ledge* is like a (a) mountain (b) damp place (c) shelf.
5. The sailboat had new *canvas.* The *canvas* was probably used for (a) windows (b) sails (c) masts.

Critical Thinking

1. What do you think of the title of the story? Exactly what is the man's problem? What is his solution to the problem?
2. Try to look at the events from "Adams'" point of view. Why does he feel that Steve deserves to die?
3. The story would be exciting even without the surprise at the end. Did you guess the ending before reading it? If so, when? If not, look back at the story and try to find clues.
4. What is your opinion of the methods used by the clergyman and the police officer to persuade "Adams" not to jump? Is there anything anyone could have said that might have been more successful? If so, what?
5. The police officer tells "Adams" that people in the crowd actually want him to jump. This is usually true of only a few people in such a crowd. They yell things like "Come on, let's show how brave you are!" Do you think such people actually want to see someone die? If not, why do they talk as they do?

Letter to the Editor

Morris Hershman

Did you ever write a "Letter to the Editor"? If not, try it sometime. If you're worried about something or have a solution for a problem in your community, you might write the editor of the local newspaper. If you have opinions on new cars, you could write the editor of an auto magazine. And if you're concerned about a mystery, you might write the editor of a mystery magazine. That is, if you still have time—and breath.

Vocabulary Preview

ARTIFICIAL RESPIRATION (ar-tuh-FISH-ul res-puh-RAY-shun) a method of helping a dying person to breathe by forcing air into and out of the lungs

• After pulling the drowning child out of the water, the lifeguard used *artificial respiration* to save the child's life.

BOARDWALK (BORD-wawk) a sidewalk made of boards

• A *boardwalk* is usually found near an ocean beach.

BUOY (BOO-ee) a floating marker in a pool, lake, river, or ocean

• The boats raced around the third *buoy* and hurried toward the finish.

COLLABORATE (kuh-LAB-uh-rayt) to work with another person on a project

• The two writers decided to *collaborate* on a book about drugs.

DISPENSARY (dis-SPEN-suh-ree) a first-aid station; a place where medicines are distributed

• The nurse's office in some schools is called the *dispensary.*

MORGUE (MORG) a place where dead bodies are kept temporarily before burial.

• "Let's take a class trip to the city *morgue,*" Heather joked.

DEAR MR. HITCHCOCK:

I'm writing to you because I've heard of you and I want your advice about something. My friends say I ought to be a real writer, anyhow. I write letters very good.

What I figure, though, is that maybe you can tell me if I ought to be as scared as I am.

Like I say, this thing really happened. If you want to make a story out of it maybe I could collaborate with you on it. I've got the story; all you'd have to do is write it up.

Anyhow, this happened to me on Brighton Beach. In Coney Island you know, in Brooklyn.

When I go out there I usually bring a blanket in a paper bag, unroll it on the sand, take off my pants and shirt and, with my bathing suit already on instead of shorts, try to catch me a little sun. I park myself near the wooden sign that says Bay 2. A lot of people near my own age come out there, in their twenties and thirties. I can lie on the sand and look up at the boardwalk. Though it's plastered with signs saying that you need shirt and pants to go walking up there, that doesn't really matter.

It happened just this afternoon, the thing I want to tell you about. You know what it's been like in the city: 93 in the shade, people dropping like flies. Even on the beach today, the sand was like hot needles under your feet.

When I'd waited for half an hour and none of my friends showed up, I went into the water. Usually I walk in up to my ankles, then dive in to get the rest of me good and wet.

Well, I swam out past the first buoy. Like all the rest of them, it's red on top. All of a sudden I saw a guy coming almost head-on into me. About twenty feet or so away I heard another man yell, "Sam!" and then there was the sound of bubbles.

The fellow had disappeared (the guy I'd been looking at —call him number one so you won't get confused) and then he showed up above water with the crook of his arm on the other guy's neck, pulling him in.

"This man's hurt!" he shouted.

I can scream pretty good, too. "Give 'em room!"

On the shore they tried artificial respiration. I went along to watch. I won't forget it as long as I live.

How long that's going to be, maybe you can guess.

Anyway, this fellow who'd brought him in stood off to one side. He wore a bright-red rubber cap and a bathing suit with white stripes at the sides. He was a beanpole of a guy, the kind who probably never stops eating, though. His large brown eyes stared right past me.

"Poor guy, whoever he was," Beanpole said to anybody who'd listen. Then he stopped and pointed. "Look!"

I did, but all I saw was the usual beach scene: the kids selling ice cream or paper cartons of orange drink or cans of cold chocolate drink. You can always recognize the sellers because they wear white sun helmets like in movies about big-game hunters in Africa.

At my left a guy wandered from girl to girl, trying to strike up a talk—"operating," it's called nowadays. A lot of acquaintances run into each other at Bay 2 because they've mostly been to the same summer places: White Roe, Banner Lodge, Tamiment, Lehman, whatever you like.

Then I saw what Beanpole had been pointing at. Two men, clearing a path for themselves, inched their way along the lines of blankets. Between them they carried what looked like a white pad folded in two. It turned out to be a stretcher.

They covered up the guy with a sheet over his face, so he couldn't even breathe.

"I guess they're taking him to the first-aid station," I said to a small blonde next to me, remembering the wooden shack on Bay 6 or 7 that looks like it was on stilts and with a staircase that takes you up to the dispensary.

The blonde shook her head slowly. "No, it's the ambulance for him and then the morgue. I saw him earlier in the day. He was a very good swimmer."

At my side the Beanpole nodded. "He must'a gotten cramps or something. We were way out, past the fourth marker. Nobody in sight except . . ." And he turned to me like he'd just noticed I was there.

I introduced myself. He mumbled that he was glad to know me, but he didn't mention his name. His eyes were hard and bright.

"How much of it did you see?" he asked quietly.

"I saw you practically on top of him and trying to get a grip on him. You did a hero's job out there. Nothing to be ashamed of, believe me!"

I had made up my mind not to go in swimming today, and when my friends came around a little later, I told them what I'd seen and spent the afternoon lying in the sun.

Once I felt somebody's eyes on me. I looked up and there was Beanpole, not too far away. He was asking a girl the name of the book she was reading, but every so often he glanced in my direction. I lay back and closed my eyes and forgot it.

But when I was going home by way of the Brighton subway, I started to ask myself questions. Once I remember I looked up at my reflection in a subway window glass; I might have been a skeleton.

Well, as soon as I got home to Snyder Avenue, where I

live, I started writing this letter to you. I was supposed to take a shower and go down to a State of Israel rally at Twenty-third and Madison, but I don't think I will. Not tonight. For all I know, maybe I'll never go to a rally again in my life.

It's this way: the blond girl at the beach told me that the dead guy was a good swimmer. If he'd been in trouble, well any old hand at swimming knows enough to float around till he can save himself. I'd heard the victim calling, "Sam!" before he went under, like Sam was right near; but Beanpole said he never knew the dead guy.

The idea I've got explains why Beanpole behaved like he did, the way he kept looking at me. I've been thinking hard, and now what I saw looks completely different. I had told Beanpole, "I saw you practically on top of him." The way I remember it now, Beanpole was holding the guy *under* water, not saving him. Beanpole kept him under water till it made no difference one way or the other.

But maybe I'm wrong. Maybe Beanpole is a right guy, after all. Maybe.

I figure it like this, though: I'm the only one who saw it happen, and he knows that.

Like I say, maybe I'm all wrong. Beanpole could have gotten so confused trying to save the guy he went around afterwards like he'd flipped his lid. He looked calm to me, but maybe some guys carry all their feelings inside them, like a guy does if he's worked up to kill somebody.

Well, that shows what you can think about in the morning. It's almost morning here, and I can look out the window and see dawn touch the rooftops across the street.

I guess I'm all wrong, crazy with the heat or whatever you'd call it.

But it'd be so easy for Beanpole to find me. After all, he knows my name and it's in the phone book. All he has to do is come in right now and shoot the top of my head off.

But even if he did the truth would come out. This letter alone is sure to do it. If I hear anybody coming, I'll stop writing and hide it as quick as I can. It'd be found by the police, afterwards. I'm sure Beanpole's name and address were taken this afternoon, and plenty of people got a good look at him.

Anyhow, that's all of it, and like I said at the beginning I want your advice about whether I'm right to be as scared as I am. Should I go to the police and tell them all this?

To show you the way a guy can get nervous; just this minute I could have sworn I felt a draft on the back of my neck, like the door had been quietly opened by somebody, and

Recall

1. The writer's trip to the beach started (a) with the excitement of going to a strange place (b) with a feeling that something would go wrong (c) in quite an ordinary way.
2. Without knowing it at the time, the writer witnessed (a) an accidental drowning (b) a murder (c) a heroic rescue.
3. "Beanpole's" real name was probably (a) Beanpole (b) Morris (c) Sam.
4. In addition to "Beanpole's" words and actions, another clue to what really happened was provided by the (a) blonde (b) lifeguard (c) writer's friends.

5. The writer started to become scared for himself (a) when the stretcher arrived (b) on his way home (c) not until he reached the last sentence of the letter.
6. Toward the end of the letter, the writer wonders if "Beanpole" (a) might try to find him (b) might go to the police (c) might help him solve the crime.

Infer

7. The end of the letter is left unfinished because the writer probably (a) went to sleep (b) decided the letter was silly (c) was killed.
8. Instead of writing the last page of the letter, the writer would probably have done better to (a) send Mr. Hitchcock a telegram (b) lock his door and call the police (c) forget about the whole thing.
9. "Beanpole's" big mistake was probably (a) staying around the beach too long (b) failing to find and destroy the letter (c) remembering the writer's name.
10. The writer seems to be (a) very, very bright (b) of average intelligence (c) hopelessly dumb.

Vocabulary Review

1. Did you ever see a *boardwalk?* A *boardwalk* is a (a) board walking (b) wide walkway (c) wooden sidewalk.

2. If involved in a bad accident, you would be glad to be taken to a (a) morgue (b) dispensary (c) buoy.
3. If you got a terrible cramp when swimming in deep water, you'd be lucky to find floating nearby a (a) morgue (b) dispensary (c) buoy.
4. If your teacher says, "I don't want anyone to *collaborate* on this composition," the teacher means you shouldn't (a) work with others (b) work by yourself (c) work too hard.
5. Helen studied *artificial respiration* in her first-aid course. Respiration has to do with (a) transportation (b) bandages (c) air.

Critical Thinking

1. Who says, "Poor guy, whoever he was"? (Look back at the story if you have to.) Is this a clue? Explain your thinking.
2. Who says, "I saw him earlier in the day. He was a very good swimmer"? (Look back if necessary.) In what way is this a clue?
3. As you were reading the story, did you begin to suspect that a murder had been committed? If so, mention the clues that tipped you off. If not, go back and find some clues.
4. In the first paragraph, the writer states, "I write letters very good." Do you agree? Find at least one example of good writing and one example of writing that might be improved. Can you find any mistakes in grammar or usage? If so, what are they?

5. What do you suppose happened after the sudden ending of the letter? Was Beanpole ever caught? Make up the details you think *most likely* to have occurred. Then write them down on a sheet of paper.

6. Suppose the experience on the beach had happened to you, and that on the way home you had started to fit the pieces of the puzzle together. What would you have done—write a letter? Call the police? Explain fully.

The Strange Guests

An old Indian legend

America's interest in the strange and the unknown did not start recently. Long, long ago, some of the earliest settlers came to our shores because they had heard stories of streets paved with gold, trees that scraped the sky, or land so rich a person could live without working. And even before that, the first Americans, the Indians, had amazing stories of their own. "The Strange Guests" is based on a tale told by the Chippewa Indians, who lived in the upper Mid-West and Canada. The story was first written down in 1837 by an unknown author.

Vocabulary Preview

COURTESY (KUR-tuh-see) polite behavior; the quality of being courteous

- It's hard to remember *courtesy* when you're angry.

FATE (FAYT) one's lot or fortune; what is fixed to happen

- Some people believe the stars govern their *fate.*

GLIMPSE (GLIMPS) a brief look

- Juan caught a *glimpse* of the airplane before it disappeared.

LAKE SUPERIOR (LAYK soo-PEER-ee-ur) the largest of the five Great Lakes, bordering Minnesota, Michigan, and Wisconsin.

- *Lake Superior* is between the United States and Canada.

LODGE (LOJ) a cabin or cottage, usually in rural areas far from cities

- Donna's mother owns a hunting *lodge* in the woods.

HUMANITY (hyoo-MAN-uh-tee) the human race; all people

- *Humanity* has always dreamed of a world without war.

OFFENSE (uh-FENTS) a rude act; a reason for hurt feelings or anger

- Jennifer is pleasant and never gives *offense* to anyone.

MANY YEARS AGO THERE LIVED, NEAR Lake Superior, an Indian hunter, who had a wife and one child. Their lodge stood in a dark part of the forest, several days' journey from the home of any other person. He spent his days hunting, and his evenings telling his wife the adventures that had come his way. Because animals were not hard to find, he seldom failed to bring home in the evening enough meat to last until the next day. And while the family was seated by the fire in their lodge, the husband talked with his wife, or sometimes told his child those tales, or taught those lessons, which all good Indians thought it necessary for everyone to know. Thus, far from all the troubles of the world, surrounded by all they thought necessary to their comfort, and happy with one another, their lives passed away happily.

The hunter had never known regret or the pain of guilt, for he was a fair and honest man. He had never broken the laws of his tribe by hunting upon the lands of his neighbors, by taking things that did not belong to him, or by any act that might anger either the village chief or the Great Spirit. He wanted only to support his family with food and skins, and to share their happiness around his cheerful fire at night. The white man had not yet taught the Indians that blankets and clothes were necessary to their comfort, or that guns could be used in the killing of animals.

The life of the Chippewa hunter flowed on peacefully.

One evening during the winter season, it happened that he remained out later than usual. His wife sat lonely in the lodge, and began to worry that he had met with some accident. Darkness had already fallen. She listened for the sound of coming footsteps; but nothing could be heard but the wind whistling around the sides of the lodge. Time passed away while she sat wondering and worrying, every moment adding to her fears and disappointment.

Suddenly she heard the sound of footsteps on the frozen snow. Not doubting that it was her husband, she quickly went to the animal skin which served as a door for the lodge. Throwing it open, she saw two strange women standing before it. Courtesy left her no time for questions. She invited the strangers to enter and warm themselves. She knew that, from the distance to the nearest neighbors, they must have walked a long way. When they had entered, she invited them to stay. They seemed to be total strangers to that part of the country. The more closely she looked at them the more curious she became.

Nothing could persuade them to come near the fire. They took their seats in a far part of the lodge. They drew their robes about them in such a manner as to almost completely hide their faces. They seemed shy and quiet, and when a glimpse could be had of their faces they looked pale, even the color of death. Their eyes were bright but deep in their heads, their cheekbones large, and their bodies slender and weak.

Seeing that her guests did not want to talk, the woman decided not to question them. She sat in silence until her husband entered. He had been led further than usual in the search for animals, but had returned with the meat of a large and fat deer. The moment he entered the lodge, the mysterious women exclaimed—

"Look what a fine and fat animal!"—and they immediately ran and pulled off pieces of the whitest fat, which they ate with their bare hands.

Such conduct seemed very strange to the hunter. But supposing the strangers had been a long time without food, he said nothing, and his wife also kept quiet.

On the following evening the same events were repeated. The hunter brought home the best parts of the animals he had killed. While he was laying them down before his wife, according to Indian ways, the two strange women came quickly up, tore off large pieces of fat, and ate them with greed. This conduct might well have made the hunter angry, but the courtesy due to strange guests made him pass over it in silence.

Knowing the parts of animals the strangers liked best, the hunter decided the next day to satisfy their wants by cutting off and tying up a piece of fat for each. This he did; and having placed the two pieces of fat upon the top of his load, as soon as he entered the lodge he gave to each stranger the part that was hers. Still the guests appeared to be hungry, and took more from the pieces lying before the wife.

Except for this unusual behavior, the conduct of the guests was courteous, although strange at times. They were quiet, modest, and careful. They kept silent and still during the day, neither speaking a word nor moving from the lodge. At night they would get up and go into the forest. There they would busy themselves picking up dry branches and pieces of trees blown down by the wind. When enough wood had been gathered to last until the next night, they carried it home upon their shoulders. Then, carefully putting the wood in its place within the lodge, they again sat down and grew silent. They were always careful to return from their work before the dawn of day, and were never known to stay out beyond that hour. The wood they gathered paid the hunter back for some of his kindness, and freed his wife from one of her most tiresome duties.

In this way, nearly the whole winter passed, every day leading to some new happening that made the guests seem a little less strange. The visitors began to appear more healthy. Their faces daily lost something of that deathly color. They improved in strength, and they slowly became a little less shy. The hunter began to hope that soon he would learn who they really were.

One evening the hunter returned very late and very tired. He laid the meat at his wife's feet. The silent women seized it and began to tear off the fat in such a greedy manner that he could no longer control his feelings of disgust. He said to himself—

"This is really too much! How can I stand it any longer?"

He did not, however, put his thought into words. But a sudden change could be seen in the two visitors. They sighed deeply and became unusually shy. They showed signs of being nervous. The good hunter immediately noticed this change and was worried that they had taken offense. As soon as he could, the husband took his wife aside. He asked whether any angry words had escaped her lips during the day. She replied that she had said nothing to give the least offense. The hunter tried to quiet his worries, but could not, for he could hear the sighs of the two strangers. Every moment added to his opinion that his guests had taken some deep offense. Finally, because he could not get this idea out of his mind, he went to the strangers and spoke to them.

"Tell me, you women, what is it that causes you pain of mind, and makes you sigh without stopping? Has anyone given you any offense during the day? Tell me, you strangers from a strange country, you women who appear not to be of this world. What it is that causes you pain of mind, and makes you sigh without stopping?"

They replied that no unkind words had ever been used towards them during their stay in the lodge. They said that they had received all the courtesy they had any right to expect.

"It is not for ourselves," they continued, "it is not for ourselves that we weep. We are weeping for the fate of humanity; we are weeping for the fate of people whom Death awaits at every moment of their existence. Proud people, whom disease attacks in youth and in age. Ordinary people, whom hunger pinches and cold makes numb. Weak people, who are born in tears, who are raised in tears, and whose whole existence is marked upon the thirsty sands of life by a line of tears. It is for these we weep.

"You have spoken truly, brother; we are not of this world. We are spirits from the land of the dead, sent upon the earth to test the living. It is not for the dead but for the living that we sigh. It was not necessary that you should have put your thoughts into words. We knew them as soon as they were in your mind. We saw that for once anger had risen in your heart. It is enough. Our trip here is ended. We came only to test you. We knew before we came that you were a kind husband, a loving father, and a good friend. But it is not alone for you we weep; it is for the fate of humanity.

"Often, very often, the husband who has lost his wife has cried, 'O Death, how cruel you are to take away my love in the spring of her youth, in the bloom of her strength! If you will permit her once more to return to my home, my thankfulness shall never end. I will raise up my voice to thank the Master of Life for such a favor. I will give my time to study how I can best make her happy while she is with me. Our lives shall roll away like a pleasant river through a flowing valley!' In this way too has the father prayed for his son, the mother for her daughter, the wife for her husband, the sister for her brother, the friend for his friend, until the cries of the living have been heard even in the land of the dead.

"The Great Spirit has finally agreed to make a test of these prayers by sending us upon the earth. He has done this to see how we should be received—coming as strangers, no one knowing from where. Three months were given to us to make the test. Now listen carefully. If, during that time, no angry thoughts had been stirred up in the place we visited, all those in the land of spirits whom their relatives had desired to return, would have been allowed to come back. More than two months have already passed, and as soon as the leaves appeared on the trees our test would have been over. It is now too late. Our trial is finished, and we are called to the pleasant fields we came from.

"Brother, it is right that one person should die to make room for another. Otherwise, the world would be filled to overflowing. It is right that the food gathered by one should be divided among others; for in the land of spirits there is neither sorrow nor hunger, neither pain nor death. Pleasant fields filled with animals spread before the eye. Every river has good fish in it, and every hill is crowned with fruit trees. It is not here, brother, but there that people begin truly to live. It is for you that are left behind that we weep.

"Brother, take our thanks for your courtesy. Fear not evil. Your luck shall still be good in the woods, and there shall always be a bright sky over your lodge. Weep not for us, for no corn will spring up from your tears."

The spirits stopped talking, but the hunter had no power over his voice to reply. While they had spoken, he had seen a glow begin to come from their faces, and a blue light had filled the lodge. As soon as they stopped, darkness slowly closed around. The hunter listened, but the voices of the spirits came no more. He heard the door of the lodge open and shut, but he never saw more of his mysterious visitors.

The success promised him was his. He became a great hunter, and never wanted anything necessary for his life. He became the father of many children, and he and his wife enjoyed health, peace, and long life.

Recall

1. Of little importance in the story is the (a) husband (b) child (c) wife.
2. The Indian family lives (a) in a city near Lake Superior (b) far from any other people (c) in a cliff dwelling.
3. To the hunter, the laws of his tribe and of his religion are (a) really important only for children (b) of little importance (c) to be obeyed.
4. The strange guests are first seen by the (a) husband (b) child (c) wife.
5. Regarding the guests, the husband and wife are (a) curious and courteous (b) curious but not courteous (c) courteous but not curious.
6. The strangest habit of the guests is (a) not talking much (b) sighing and weeping every day (c) eating fat greedily.
7. As time passes, the guests become (a) even stranger (b) a little more at home (c) even paler.
8. It is the Indian hunter's way to lay pieces of the animals he has killed (a) in front of his guests (b) on the fire (c) before his wife.
9. The guests help the Indian family by (a) looking for roots and berries (b) gathering wood (c) chewing on animal skins.
10. The test is over when the hunter (a) asks his guests to leave (b) says an angry word (c) thinks an angry thought.
11. The hunter finally questions the guests because (a) their sighs bother him (b) his wife insists on it (c) his family is getting too little to eat.
12. The guests explain that they are weeping for (a) themselves (b) the Indian family (c) all humanity.

13. The strange guests say they have been sent by (a) an Indian chief (b) the Great Spirit (c) the U.S. Bureau of Indian Affairs.
14. If the husband and wife had passed the test, (a) they would have been taken immediately to the home of the strange guests (b) corn would have grown from their tears (c) some of the dead would have been returned to life.
15. The story shows that the Chippewa Indians believed in something like a (a) heaven (b) hell (c) democratic form of government.

Infer

16. The story seems to show (a) the influence of the white man on the Indians (b) the Indians as they really were (c) almost nothing about Indian life and beliefs.
17. The story indicates that the Chippewa Indians placed a high value on (a) women's rights (b) cleanliness of food (c) courtesy to guests.
18. The story indicates that it is the fate of most people to be (a) sad (b) happy (c) jealous.
19. The story suggests that if a person tries hard he can be (a) cruel when necessary (b) perfect (c) very good but not perfect.
20. Another good title for the story might be (a) "Everyday Life Among the Indians" (b) "A Test for Humanity" (c) "Guess Who's Coming to Dinner!"

Vocabulary Review

Write on your paper the word in *italics* that belongs in each blank. Use each word only once.

courtesy	*glimpse*	*humanity*
fate	*lodge*	*offense*

1. Do you believe a fortuneteller really knows what your——— will be?
2. The old man lived alone in a ——— in the woods.
3. Milagros' grandmother will be remembered for her kindness and ——— to all people.
4. The flash of lightning gave Leroy a ——— of the road ahead of him.
5. Pete took ——— when I told him his hair needed washing.
6. Does the United Nations really represent the interests of all ———?

Critical Thinking

1. Describe at least two Indian customs mentioned in the story.
2. Describe the religious beliefs mentioned in the story.
3. By the standards of most people today, the Indian husband and his wife are presented as *impossibly* good people.

They spend over two months with the strange guests before one of them has an angry or selfish thought. Do you believe this is possible—even for good people? Explain.

4. Treating strangers well was a custom in many Indian tribes. What use do you think this custom served?

5. Briefly explain what you think the story says about life and death.

The Provençal Tale

Ann Radcliffe

Did you ever wonder who invented the modern horror story? Who was the first to dip a pen in blood and write tales of pure terror? That honor belongs to Ann Radcliffe (1764-1823). The wife of an English newspaper editor, Mrs. Radcliffe escaped an otherwise quiet life by letting her imagination lead her to the unknown. The tale that follows is from her most famous book, The Mysteries of Udolpho *(1794). Read it carefully—and take a deep breath before the last page.*

Vocabulary Preview

BARON (BAIR-un) a lord or nobleman; a person of high rank
• The king asked the *baron* to meet with him in the castle.

GHASTLY (GAST-lee) dreadful, horrible, terrifying
• The monster had seven *ghastly* stitches in his forehead.

MAGNIFICENCE (mag-NIF-uh-sunts) splendor; greatness; amazing beauty and size
• The *magnificence* of the queen's palace surprised all who saw it.

PACED (PAYST) walked back and forth across
• Sally *paced* the floor while waiting for the phone to ring.

PASSAGE (PAS-ij) a path or corridor
• An alley is a narrow *passage* between two buildings.

PROVENÇAL (pro-vun-SAL) referring to Provence, a region in southern France
• Old *Provençal* stories often tell of life in the 1200's.

PROVINCE (PROV-ints) an area; a section of a country
• In some countries, what we call a state is called a *province*.

THERE ONCE LIVED, IN THE PROVINCE OF Bretagne, a noble baron, famous for his riches and his kindness to guests. His castle was more splendid than those of many kings. Beautiful ladies and brave knights came from far-off countries to feast in the great hall of his castle. The baron's eight musicians, the banners that waved along the roof, the huge paintings, the gold and silver dishes, the piles of tasty food, the costly uniforms of the many servants—all combined to form a scene of magnificence such as we may not hope to see in these dull modern days.

The following adventure is told about the baron. One night, having stayed late at the dinner table, he went to his bedroom. A few minutes after he had told his servants to go, he was surprised by the sudden appearance of a man he had never before seen. The stranger's face was sorrowful. The baron believed this person had been hiding in his apartment, since he could hardly have just entered without being seen. Calling loudly to his servants, the baron drew his sword, which he had not yet removed from his belt. The stranger, slowly moving forward, told him that there was nothing to fear. He had come in friendship, he said, and wanted only to disclose a terrible secret, which it was necessary for the baron to know.

The baron was impressed by the polite manner of the stranger, and looked at him for some time in silence. Then he returned his sword to his belt, and asked how the man had gotten into the apartment, and the purpose of his unusual visit.

The stranger said he could not then explain himself. But,

if the baron would follow him to the edge of the forest a short distance from the castle, he would there prove to him that he had something important to communicate.

This suggestion alarmed the baron again. He could hardly believe that the stranger meant to take him to such a lonely spot, at this hour of the night, without planning to kill him. He refused to go. He stated that if the stranger were up to any good, he would here and now explain the reason for his visit.

While the baron spoke this, he examined the stranger still more carefully than before. But he noticed no change in his face, nor anything that might hint at an evil plan. His visitor was dressed like a knight. He was tall and proud, and had polite manners. Still, however, the stranger refused to tell the reason for his visit in any place but the one he had mentioned. At the same time he gave hints about the secret. Finally the baron grew curious enough to agree to the stranger's request.

"Sir knight," said he, "I will go with you to the forest, and will take with me only four of my servants."

To this, however, the knight objected.

"What I want to communicate," said he seriously, "is for you alone. There are only three living persons to whom the secret is known. It is of more importance to you than you realize. In future years, you will look back to this night with satisfaction or sorrow, depending on what you now do. If you would be happy in the future, follow me. I promise you on my honor as a knight that no evil shall come to you. If you are content to doubt me, remain here in your room, and I will leave as I came."

"Sir knight," replied the baron, "how is it possible that my future peace can depend upon what I decide now?"

"That is not now to be told," said the stranger. "I will explain myself no more. It is late. If you follow me it must be quickly."

The baron paced his room for some time in silence. He was impressed by the words of the stranger. But the unusual request he feared to agree to, and feared also to refuse. At length he said, "Sir knight, you are completely unknown to me. Tell me yourself, does it make sense that I should trust myself alone with a stranger, at this hour, in the forest? Tell me, at least, who you are, and who helped you hide yourself in this room."

The knight frowned at these words, and was a moment silent. Then, with a stern look, he said, "I am an English knight. I am called Sir Bevys of Lancaster, and my deeds are not unknown in the world. I was returning to my native land, when night fell in the forest."

"Your name is not unknown to fame" said the baron. "I have heard of it. But why, since my castle is known to entertain all passing knights, didn't you come to my gate? Why didn't you appear at the feast, where you would have been welcomed? Why did you choose to hide yourself in my castle, and sneak into my room at midnight?"

The stranger frowned, and turned away in silence. But the baron repeated the questions.

"I come not," said the knight, "to answer questions, but to communicate facts. If you want to know more, follow me. Again I give you the honor of a knight that you shall return in safety. Be quick to decide—I must be gone."

After thinking some more, the baron decided to follow the stranger, and to see the result of his unusual request. He therefore drew his sword, and taking a lamp, told the knight to lead on. The stranger obeyed. Opening the door, they passed into another room, where the baron was surprised to find his servants asleep. He was about to punish them for their carelessness, when the knight waved his hand and shook his head, and they passed on.

The knight, having gone down a staircase, opened a secret door, which the baron had believed was known only to himself. They proceeded through several narrow and winding passages. At last they came to a small gate that opened beyond the walls of the castle. Noticing that these secret passages were well known to the stranger, the baron wondered if he shouldn't turn back. Didn't the adventure now promise some danger? Then, remembering that he carried his sword, and noticing again the polite and noble manner of his guest, he regained his courage. He blushed that it had failed him for a moment.

He now found himself on the great steps before the gates of his castle. Looking up, he saw lights shining in the windows of the guests, who were now going to bed. As he shivered in the wind and looked on the dark scene around him, he thought of the comfort of his warm room and his cheerful fire.

The wind was strong, and the baron watched his lamp carefully, expecting every moment to see it go out. But though the flame grew dim, it did not disappear. He continued to follow the stranger, who often sighed as he went, but did not speak.

When they reached the edge of the forest, the knight turned and raised his head, as if he meant to say something. But then, closing his lips, in silence he walked on.

As they entered the dark woods, the baron, now worried again, wondered whether to go on. He asked how much farther they were to go. The knight replied only by waving his hand, and the baron, with slow steps and a suspicious eye, followed through a dark and difficult path. When they had gone quite a way, he again demanded where they were going. This time he refused to walk another step unless he was told. As he said this, he looked at his sword, and then at the knight.

"A little farther is the place where I would lead you," said the stranger. "No evil shall come to you—I have promised on my honor as a knight."

The baron, feeling better, again followed in silence. They soon arrived at a deep valley in the forest, where the dark trees entirely shut out the sky. The knight sighed deeply as he walked on, and sometimes paused. Finally he reached a spot where the trees crowded into a knot. Here he turned, and with a terrific look, pointed to the ground. The baron saw there the body of a man, stretched out at length and swimming in blood. A ghastly wound was on the forehead, and death appeared already to have changed the face.

The baron, on seeing this sight, drew back in horror. He looked at the knight for explanation. Then he started to lift the body, to see if there were any remains of life. But the stranger, waving his hand, gave him so sad a look that he stopped.

But what were the baron's feelings next! Holding the lamp near the head of the corpse, the baron discovered the exact face of the stranger—at whom he now looked up in surprise and shock. As he stared, he saw the face of the knight change and begin to fade. Soon the stranger's whole form slowly vanished before him. While the baron stood fixed to the spot, a voice was heard to say these words:

"The body of Sir Bevys of Lancaster, a noble knight of England, lies before you. He was this night robbed and murdered as he journeyed towards his native land. Respect the honor of knighthood, and the laws of all lands. Bury the body in your castle ground, and cause his murderers to be punished. If you do this, peace and happiness shall be with you and your court forever!"

The baron, when he recovered from the shock into which this adventure had thrown him, returned to his castle. Soon the body of Sir Bevys was carried from the forest. On the following day it was buried, with the honors of knighthood, in the chapel of the castle, attended by all the noble knights and ladies who were the guests of the great Baron de Brunne.

Recall

1. At the beginning of the story, we are told that the baron was famous chiefly for his (a) interest in mystery (b) courage (c) kindness to guests.
2. The baron's first reaction to the stranger was to be (a) afraid (b) kind (c) amused.
3. The mysterious visitor turned out to be quite (a) rude (b) polite (c) dishonest.
4. When the stranger first stated his request, the baron was (a) eager to help (b) angered beyond belief (c) afraid and curious.
5. The baron refused at first to go with his visitor because he (a) already knew the visitor's secret (b) was worried about his life (c) felt very sleepy.
6. When he finally went with the knight, the baron took (a) four servants (b) a map of the forest (c) a lamp and a sword.
7. The baron became even more disturbed when the knight seemed to know (a) the castle's secret passages (b) the servants' names (c) the baron's middle name.
8. During the trip through the forest, the baron (a) led the way (b) lost his sword (c) had moments of doubt.
9. At the end of the trip, the baron (a) saw the body of a man (b) imagined he saw the body of a man (c) killed the stranger.
10. The visitor differed from the dead man in having (a) heavier clothes (b) no ghastly wound on his forehead (c) a secret ring.
11. The big mystery in the story concerns how a person can at the same time be (a) young and old (b) rich and poor (c) dead and alive.
12. The stranger asked the baron to do two things: bury his body and (a) visit his family in England (b) punish his murderers (c) tell the story of the strange adventure.

Infer

13. The reason the stranger did not tell the baron his secret was probably that (a) he wanted to play a joke on the baron (b) he himself wasn't sure what the secret was (c) the baron wouldn't have believed it.
14. The reason the servants did not answer the baron's call when he first saw the stranger was probably that they were (a) asleep (b) afraid (c) off duty.
15. In convincing the baron to come with him, the stranger made most use of the baron's (a) sense of fair play (b) anger (c) curiosity.
16. Most of the baron's actions in the story were done (a) to prove the stranger wrong (b) to discover the stranger's secret (c) to save the stranger's life.
17. The knight could not have attended the evening feast because he was (a) unwelcome (b) dead (c) in England.
18. The author wants you to believe that the dead body (a) first appeared when the baron saw it (b) left its place to appear in the baron's room (c) lay in the forest throughout the story.
19. It is clear from the story that its author, Ann Radcliffe, (a) was insane (b) believed in ghosts (c) knew how to build up suspense.
20. A good title for the story might be (a) "The Secret of Sir Bevys" (b) "The Secret Passage" (c) "A Knight's Night Out."

Vocabulary Review

1. Dean's family visited the western *provinces* of Canada. *Provinces* mean (a) forests (b) capitals (c) sections.
2. Aaron's *ghastly* dream woke him up. *Ghastly* means (a) sad (b) horrible (c) glorious.
3. The *baron* led his soldiers into battle. A *baron* is a (a) general (b) leader (c) nobleman.

4. A short *passage* led from the apartment to the street. *Passage* means (a) guide or monitor (b) path or corridor (c) row of lights.
5. Mr. Zenovich *paced* the floor. *Paced* means (a) walked back and forth on (b) washed carefully (c) measured exactly.
6. The *magnificence* of the queen's jewels caused everyone to gasp in wonder. *Magnificence* means great (a) beauty (b) shape (c) cleanliness.

Critical Thinking

1. Explain how the following words describe the baron at different points in the story: *fearful, curious, suspicious, angry, terrified.*

2. What does the story tell about life in the Middle Ages? Who would you rather be, yourself today or the baron about the year 1200? Yourself or the baron's servant? Explain.

3. "The Provençal Tale" was written almost two hundred years ago. The story itself tells of events which took place even earlier, in the Middle Ages. But couldn't a similar story be told about modern characters? Suppose you were given the job of turning "The Provençal Tale" into a ghost story for TV. What type of person in modern America would be most like a baron of the Middle Ages? An oil millionaire? A senator? A rock superstar? What could you substitute for the role of the knight? What other changes would you need to make in the story? Write down your ideas on a sheet of paper.

4. In the Middle Ages, the knights were a highly respected group of people. About fifty years ago, a public opinion survey showed that successful business people—the "giants of industry"—were the most respected group in America. About twenty years ago, another survey gave this honor to U.S. Senators. In your opinion, what group of people today deserves the most respect? Explain your answer.

The Gods' Gift to Chang Fu-Yen

An Eighth-Century Chinese Tale

Ready for a trip? Now we go halfway around the world and back to the year 750. The strange story you're about to read was first told in ancient China about twelve hundred years ago. Today it's hard to imagine how cruel life was in the China of ages past. As you'll discover, most of the people were terribly poor. They often went hungry. Some died of starvation, while others sold themselves into slavery so that their families could eat. Yet in some ways, life in old China was not too different from our own. It was considered very, very important for children to love and respect their parents. And as this story proves, the people enjoyed tales of horror and the supernatural.

Vocabulary Preview

EMBRACED (em-BRAYST) hugged, threw one's arms around someone
- The Russian men *embraced* when they met each other.

MERCHANT (MUR-chunt) a person who makes a living by buying and selling
- A jewel *merchant* bought the ring for $500.

SOIL (SOYL) earth; the material in which plants grow
- Mr. Jablonski found some good *soil* to place in his flowerpots.

STARVATION (star-VAY-shun) death caused by lack of food
- The pioneers faced *starvation* when their food ran out.

LONG, LONG AGO, IN THE HILLS OF CHINA, there lived a boy named Chang Fu-Yen. We know almost nothing of his early life. At five years of age, it seems, he became engaged to marry another child, Ying Ying T'ien. The marriage was planned by the children's parents. As was the custom, Chang and Ying Ying were not supposed to see each other until their wedding.

All in all, we must suppose that as a boy Chang was both good and happy. A bad boy would never have been rewarded in later years by the gods, and in truth Chang had little reason to be sad. His father, Wang, was a farmer. The family's farm was just small enough to be cared for by the family. And it was just large enough to grow food for the family—until the coming of the Great Hunger.

Chang Fu-Yen was sixteen when the Great Hunger started. After the showers of spring, no rain at all came to the hills of China. All summer long, they carried water to the fields from a small river over two miles down the valley. With hard work, they were able to carry enough water to grow food for the following winter. It was not the best food, and there were never second helpings. But it was something to eat, and the family ate better than most. That was the winter when people from farms all over China crowded into the cities, to search for work that wasn't there and for food that couldn't be found.

Wang waited eagerly for the spring rains to bring water to the land. Finally the rains came. One evening Wang stood in front of his cottage. He smiled as he watched a gray curtain of rain come over the western mountains. It moved closer, closer, and closer to the family farm. The happy cries of neighbors echoed back and forth across the valley. Suddenly the rain started to fall on the farm. Wang sat down on a stone and let the rain fall on his smiling face until dark. It had been almost a year. Now the rains had come.

But too much rain fell in too short a time. In a few days, the rich, black earth turned to mud. Then the mud became muddy water, which flowed down the hillside and off the farm.

The following summer was worse than ever. No rain fell. The earth looked like brick. The family had planted rice and beans in the little soil that had not been washed off the farm. But the sun dried the soil almost as fast as the family could water it.

Now the family faced slow death by starvation. The first to go was Chang's mother. She fell to the ground as she walked along carrying two pails of water. She had almost reached the farm when she laid down her life, and she was careful to the end. Her pails were put down so that not a drop of water was wasted.

"The gods have been kind to your mother," said Wang to his son. "A quick death is the best ending a life can have, except maybe the sweet dreams that come when one freezes to death. Your mother is happy now, and she has avoided the pains of hunger."

Thoughts like these made Chang feel better about his mother. But they did nothing to lighten the other sorrows that pressed upon his heart. Death, he thought, was an ugly word. Whatever else it meant, it always meant an end to life.

But life has a way of going on. Soon Wang and his son went back to carrying water and caring for the small strips of sun-baked soil. Neither of them ever said a word about what was becoming clearer with every passing day. There would not be enough food to last all winter. There would be food for half the winter, maybe, or a little longer. But not enough to last until the spring showers again brought life to the soil.

One afternoon, in the early part of the winter, Chang went hunting in the snow-covered mountains west of the farm. When he returned, he found his father full of good news. Wang looked happier than he had in months.

"Help has come at last," Wang said, throwing his arms around his son's shoulders. "My cousin, a shoemaker in Hankow, came here while you were gone. There is work in his shop for one of us. Two later on, but one now. So I will go, and send for you when I can."

The next morning, Chang watched his father pack a few clothes and leave for Hankow. When Wang had passed out of sight, Chang followed him in his mind—down out of the hills to the great Yangtze River, then east on a boat for many miles to the city of Hankow.

At first Chang was lonely in his new life. He lived from day to day, waiting for word to join his father. The Great Hunger had changed many things. Chang's mother had died, his father had gone to Hankow, and Chang himself was soon to leave the farm, probably for good. If the Great Hunger had never come, Chang would not have been allowed to see Ying Ying until their wedding, even though she lived less than a mile away. But now things were different. No one knew who would live and who would die. No one cared if Chang and Ying Ying saw each other.

After Wang left for Hankow, Chang and Ying Ying met by accident. Soon Chang was spending much of his time at the T'iens'. He grew to love Ying Ying as they sat under the stars and talked about the life they might have had together.

Both of them wondered how their parents had known that the two five-year-olds were meant for each other.

That winter there was little that Chang could do on the farm. Snow covered the ground, and everything was frozen hard. When he was not with Ying Ying, he spent most of his time hunting in the mountains. He shot almost nothing, for in the second year of the Great Hunger there were few animals left to shoot. But he did find something in the snow that was to bring a sudden change to his life.

What he found was the frozen body of his father.

At once Chang knew the truth. There had been no job in a shoemaker's shop. There had been no cousin in Hankow. His father had not even gone to Hankow. He had walked up into the mountains to die, so that his son might have enough food to live until spring.

"My father gave his life for mine," said Chang Fu-Yen. "Now I will give my life for his memory."

Three weeks later, Chang was seated in the crowded market place of Hankow. Around him were many merchants, selling everything from furniture to pots, from rugs to pigs. But Chang was selling none of these things. He was selling himself.

Though it was cold, Chang had stripped himself to the waist. He wanted the people who passed to see how strong he was. He sat cross-legged, with his back against a post. Above his head was a sign he had painted himself: *Slave for Sale—100 Gold Pieces.*

Most of the people in the market place that morning never noticed Chang. The few people who did shook their heads when they read the sign. "A hundred gold pieces for a slave!" they laughed. "It is far too much."

Chang became sad, cold, and angry as the hours passed. He knew that no one would buy a slave with an angry face, so he sat staring at the ground. Feet passed before his eyes—the many bare feet of the poor, and the few shoe-covered feet of the rich. Suddenly he found himself looking at a pair of shoes of the finest red leather. He knew they belonged to a very rich person.

"This is a good strong slave," Chang heard a voice say. "But the price is too high. Who is your owner, boy? I want to see him about the price."

Chang's eyes traveled upward. They came to rest on a small, round, wrinkled face. The gentleman was surely a rich merchant. No one else would be dressed this way.

"I am my own owner," Chang told the merchant. "I am free to sell myself."

"Selling yourself!" said the merchant. "You must need money very badly."

"I do," Chang replied. "I must give my father the best funeral that money can buy." Then he told the merchant the sad story of what the Great Hunger had done to his family.

The merchant bent forward. "There is nothing better than for a son to love and honor his parents," he told Chang. "But, suppose I did buy you. Suppose I gave you a hundred gold pieces, and sent you off to bury your father. How would I know you would ever return?"

Chang looked the merchant in the eye. "You know I will come back because I tell you so," he stated. "The son of Wang does not tell you a lie."

The merchant agreed to buy Chang. He took the boy to his shop and showed him the work he would be doing, weaving and selling fancy silk. Then he gave Chang a leather bag that held a hundred gold coins. "Be back in a month," he ordered. "I do not have to tell you what happens to a slave who runs away."

Chang knew the punishment—death. Promising to be

back in a month, he ran off to find a boat sailing up the Yangtze River. In two weeks he was home, and a few days later his father's frozen body was brought down from the mountains. He planned the funeral with care. Four white horses were to pull the coffin to the cemetery. Flowers could not be bought in the winter, so Chang had hundreds made out of paper. And the fine funeral went as planned—except for one thing.

When the T'ien family arrived, Ying Ying was not among them. Chang was sad. He had looked forward to seeing Ying Ying, if only to tell her good-bye for the last time. And he was even more unhappy when he heard that Ying Ying was sick in bed. "She is very ill, Chang," her father said. "For a month she has been sinking slowly. There is little hope."

After the funeral, Chang spoke to no one. He stared down at his feet as he walked back to the river. Then he got into the boat that would carry him back to Hankow, and back to slavery. He sat down in the boat, his elbows on his knees, his face in his hands. Behind him he was leaving his father dead, his mother dead, and his Ying Ying about to die. The boat started to move without his knowing it.

Suddenly, for some reason, he found himself listening to the sound of feet running along the river bank. "Chang!" came a voice. "Chang Fu-Yen!"

It was Ying Ying, looking better than ever! She took a running jump and landed beside Chang in the boat. Soon her face was in Chang's hands. Chang sat blinking at the roses on her cheeks, and the hope in her eyes.

"I'm going with you!" said Ying Ying.

"But I'm a slave!" cried Chang. "I'm not free to marry. You know that."

"Of course I know that," replied Ying Ying. "That's why I'm going. You see, I have a plan."

"A plan? What?" Chang asked.

But Ying Ying would tell him nothing. When they reached Hankow, Ying Ying went her own way. It was two weeks before she came to the shop where Chang was working.

She came at a time when the merchant was off on a trip. With her she brought a beautiful green silk robe. On the back was a huge dragon's head. It had a shiny sea-colored face, a bright red and yellow tongue, and jewels for eyes.

"This is wonderful!" Chang said, holding up the robe. "We have nothing like it here in the shop. Where did you get it?"

"I made it," Ying Ying said proudly. "And I know what it's worth. The silk merchant will gladly give you a gold piece for it. But you are not to take the gold. Let the merchant keep it. I will make ninety-nine more robes, and then you will be free to marry me."

Three years later, three things happened on the same day. Robe number one hundred was finished, Chang became a free man, and he and Ying Ying were married. They opened a small silk shop of their own. In a few months they had saved enough money to visit Ying Ying's parents.

This trip up the great Yangtze River was very different for Chang. Now he went as a free man, dressed in a good silk suit, with a happy young woman at his side. When he stepped off the boat, he hired a carriage to take them to Ying Ying's old home.

The Great Hunger was now a thing of the past. The fields were green, and the trees were heavy. Ying Ying broke into tears when she saw her old house. She had not dared to write home since the day she had jumped out of her sick bed and run all the way to the river. She had been afraid that her parents would make her come home. Now she asked Chang to go into the house first. She didn't want to surprise them by walking in suddenly.

Ying Ying's father welcomed Chang as if the young man had been his own son. "Come," he said when they had greeted each other, "my sick daughter Ying Ying has talked about you for three years."

"What!" cried Chang. "Ying Ying is with me! She waits in the carriage!"

When the young woman who had been sick for three years heard these words, she got up from her bed and put on a robe. She reached the door of the house just as the other Ying Ying stepped from the carriage. For a moment the two Ying Yings stood looking at each other—the one pale and weak, the other glowing with life. Then, before the eyes of all, they ran toward each other, embraced, and joined together in becoming one body.

A single, surprised Ying Ying now stood before her parents and her husband. She was wearing the clothes of both Ying Yings. It was easy to take off one set of clothes. But ever after she carried two sets of memories.

We can understand why people in China talked of this for many years. Ying Ying and Chang, however, said very little, even to each other. They knew that what had happened had something to do with loving one's parents. But they were wise enough not to question too closely a gift of the gods.

Recall

1. Chang was engaged when he was (a) five (b) about sixteen (c) in Hankow working.
2. Wang provided for his family by working (a) in a shoemaker's shop (b) in a silk merchant's shop (c) on a small farm.
3. The Great Hunger was caused by (a) a war (b) insects (c) the weather.
4. The first to die was (a) Chang's father (b) Chang's mother (c) Ying Ying.
5. Chang discovered his father's lie when (a) it was first told (b) Wang's body was found (c) Chang himself got to Hankow.
6. Chang and Ying Ying finally met (a) on the day they were married (b) when Chang was a slave (c) during the Great Hunger.
7. Chang sold himself into slavery to (a) get money to marry Ying Ying (b) pay for his father's farm (c) give his father a fine funeral.
8. The plan that finally freed Chang from slavery was (a) his own (b) the merchant's (c) Ying Ying's.
9. While in Hankow, Ying Ying had not written home because she (a) disliked her parents (b) feared her parents would come to get her (c) didn't know how to write.
10. When the two Ying Ying's embraced each other, they (a) talked about their different lives (b) exchanged clothes (c) became one person.
11. The character who carried two sets of memories was (a) the merchant (b) Ying Ying (c) Chang.
12. Which of the following events happened first? (a) Ying Ying made robe number one hundred (b) Chang and

Ying Ying met each other for the first time (c) Chang began working in Hankow.

13. Which of the following events happened last? (a) Chang sold himself as a slave (b) Ying Ying made robe number one hundred (c) Chang buried his father.

Infer

14. When his wife died, Wang said, "A quick death is the best ending a life can have, except maybe the sweet dreams that come when one freezes to death." Later in the story this sentence also applies to (a) Ying Ying's illness (b) Wang's own death (c) Chang's cold feeling as he sat in the market place.
15. Ying Ying joins Chang in the boat going to Hankow because she (a) wants to get away from her parents (b) is curious about city life (c) loves Chang and wants to help him.
16. At the end of the story, Ying Ying seems to be (a) as surprised as anyone by the strange events (b) only pretending surprise (c) hoping her trick will fool her parents.
17. "He smiled as he watched a gray curtain of rain come over the western mountains." A word in this sentence used in an unusual way is (a) *smiled* (b) *watched* (c) *curtain.*
18. The story suggests that the ancient Chinese placed a high value on (a) scientific farming (b) individual freedom (c) honoring one's parents.

19. The story is a little unusual because it has no (a) beginning, middle, and end (b) heros (c) villains.

20. The story suggests that sometimes (a) bad acts are punished (b) good acts are rewarded (c) slavery has its good points.

Vocabulary Review

1. With plenty of water, desert *soil* will grow good crops. *Soil* means (a) workers (b) heat (c) earth.

2. *Starvation* is rare in the United States. *Starvation* means death from (a) hard work (b) hunger (c) accident.

3. The woman *embraced* her lost child. *Embraced* means (a) scolded (b) found (c) hugged.

4. The *merchant* sold three diamond rings. A *merchant* is a (a) business person (b) city person (c) politician.

Critical Thinking

1. What attitude was a child in old China supposed to have toward his parents? Why might this attitude have been necessary for the well-being of families at that time and place?

2. Today we are surprised at the idea of parents making decisions about marriage for their small children. Why do you think the custom developed? In what way might it have been useful? harmful?

3. In the story Wang tells a lie for what he thinks is a good reason. What is the lie? Would you have told it? Why or why not? Try to outline a situation in which it might be necessary for someone to tell a lie.

4. Today some people suppose that women in ancient times never did anything important. How does the story show this belief to be false?

5. Explain the last sentence of the story in your own words.

The Tell-Tale Heart

Edgar Allan Poe

No book called Tales of Mystery and the Unknown *would be complete without a story by the strange American genius, Edgar Allan Poe. Born in 1809, Poe never knew his father, an actor who left his family and simply disappeared. Death claimed Poe's mother when he was two, and the years that followed brought him periods of poverty, hunger, insanity, and alcoholism. Death fascinated Poe; death became his life as a writer. In Poe's stories, people are buried alive and spirits of the dead return to take over the bodies of the living. He piles horror upon horror, corpse upon corpse. Poe himself was found near death on a street in Baltimore, Maryland, in 1849; four days later he was gone. The mystery surrounding his death remains unknown.*

Vocabulary Preview

DISTINCT (dis-STINKT) clear; easily seen, heard or understood

• An actor must speak in a *distinct* way to be heard at the rear of a large theater.

FILM (FILM) a thin covering or coating

• The puddle had a thin *film* of ice on it.

HIDEOUS (HID-ee-us) horribly ugly or frightening

• The picture of the *hideous* witch frightened little Tim.

INSTINCT (IN-stinkt) a natural or "built-in" feeling or guide to action

• New-born babies do not have to be taught how to drink milk. They know what to do naturally, by *instinct.*

MUFFLED (MUF-uld) covered or wrapped up, to cut down on sound

• The doctor's face mask *muffled* her voice a little.

VICTIM (VIK-tim) a person who suffers from a crime

• Ms. Schmidt, the murderer's second *victim,* was shot in the head.

VILLAIN (VIL-un) a "bad person"; a criminal

• The *villain* who shot Ms. Schmidt remains on the loose.

VULTURE (VUL-chur) a large, ugly bird

• A *vulture* will eat meat that is nearly rotten.

TRUE!—NERVOUS—VERY, VERY HORRIBLY nervous I had been and am; but why *will* you say that I am a madman? The disease had sharpened my five senses—not destroyed—not dulled them. Above all was my sense of hearing sharp. I heard all things in the heavens and on the earth. I heard many things in hell. How, then, am I a madman? Listen, and see how clearly—how calmly I can tell you the whole story.

It is impossible to say how the idea first entered my brain; but once I thought of it, it haunted me day and night. There was no good reason. There was no real hatred. I loved the old man. He had never done me any wrong. He had never insulted me. For his gold I had no desire. I think it was his eye! Yes, it was this! One of his eyes looked like a vulture's —a pale blue eye, with a film over it. Whenever it fell upon me, my blood ran cold; and so—very gradually—I made up my mind to take the life of the old man, and thus get rid of that eye for ever.

Now this is the point. You believe me mad. Madmen know nothing. But you should have seen *me.* You should have seen how wisely I proceeded—with what care—with what planning I went to work! I was never kinder to the old man than during the whole week before I killed him. And every night, about midnight, I turned the knob of his door and opened it—oh, so gently! And then, when I had made an opening big enough for my head, I put in a dark lantern, all closed, closed, so that no light came out, and then I put in my head. Oh, you would have laughed to see how carefully I put my head in! I moved it slowly—very, very slowly, so that I might not disturb the old man's sleep. It took me an hour to move my head so far that I could see him as he lay upon his bed. Ha!—would a madman have been so wise as this? And then, when my head was well in the room, I undid the lantern carefully—oh, so carefully—carefully (for the hinges squeaked)— I undid it just so much that a single thin ray fell upon the vulture eye. And this I did for seven long nights—every night just at midnight—but I found the eye always closed; and so it was impossible to do the work; for it was not the old man who troubled me, but his Evil Eye. And every morning, when the daylight came, I went right into the bedroom, and spoke to him, calling him by name in a cheerful tone, and asking how he had slept that night. So you see he would have been a very unusual old man, indeed, to suspect that every night, just at twelve, I looked in upon him while he was asleep.

On the eighth night I was more careful than ever in opening the door. A watch's minute hand moves more quickly than did mine. Never before that night had I really *felt* all of my own powers—my own wisdom. I could hardly hold in my feelings of joy. To think that there I was opening the door, little by little, and he not even dreaming of my secret thoughts. I laughed a little at the idea; and perhaps he heard me, for he moved on the bed suddenly, as if frightened. Now you may think that I drew back—but no. His room was as black as tar with the thick darkness (for the shades were fastened, for fear of robbers), and so I knew that he could not see the opening of the door, and I kept pushing on steadily, steadily.

I had my head in, and was about to open the lantern, when my thumb slipped on the tin, and the old man sprang up in the bed crying out—"Who's there?"

I kept quite still and said nothing. For a whole hour I did not move a muscle, and in the meantime I did not hear him lie down. He was still sitting up in the bed, listening.

In a little while I heard a slight groan, and I knew it was the groan of pure terror. It was not a groan of pain or of sadness—oh, no!—it was the low muffled sound that comes from the bottom of the soul when overfilled with fear. I knew the sound well. Many a night, just at midnight, when all the world slept, it has come up from my own chest, deepening, with a dreadful echo, the terrors that bothered me. I say I knew it well. I knew what the old man felt, and I pitied him, although I laughed at heart. I knew that he had been lying awake ever since the first slight noise, when he had turned in the bed. His fears had been ever since growing upon him. He had been trying to find good reasons for his fear but could not. He had been saying to himself—"It is nothing but the wind in the chimney—it is only a mouse crossing the floor." Yes, he had been trying to comfort himself with these explanations; but he had found it useless. Useless; because Death, in drawing near him, had walked with his black shadow before him, and captured the victim. And it was the unseen shadow that caused him to feel—although he neither saw nor heard—to *feel* the nearness of my head within the room.

When I had waited a long time, very patiently, without hearing him lie down, I decided to open the lantern a little—a very, very little crack. So I opened it—you cannot imagine how slowly, slowly—until a single dim ray, like the thread of the spider, shot out from the crack and full upon the vulture eye.

It was open—wide, wide open—and I grew furious as I looked upon it. I saw it so clearly—all a dull blue, with a hideous film over it that chilled my very bones; but I could see nothing else of the old man's face or body; for I had pointed the ray as if by instinct, exactly upon the damned spot.

Have I not told you that what you mistake for madness is nothing but the unusual power of my senses?—now, I say, there came to my ears a low, dull, quick sound, such as a watch makes when surrounded by cotton. I knew *that* sound well too. It was the beating of the old man's heart. It increased my anger, as the beating of a drum increases a soldier's courage.

But even yet I held back and kept still. I scarcely breathed. I held the lantern motionless. I tried to see how steadily I could keep the ray upon the eye. Meantime the hellish drum beat of the heart increased. It grew quicker and quicker, and louder and louder every instant. The old man's terror *must* have been great! It grew louder, I say, louder every moment!—do you hear me well? I have told you that I am nervous: so I am. And now at the dead hour of the night, in the dreadful silence of that old house, so strange a noise as this excited me to terror I could not control. Yet, for some minutes longer I held back and stood still. But the beating grew louder, louder! I thought the heart must burst. And now a new worry seized me—the sound would be heard by a neighbor! The old man's hour had come! With a loud yell, I threw open the lantern and leaped into the room. He shrieked loudly once—once only. In an instant I dragged him to the floor, and pulled the heavy bed over him. I then smiled, to find my job so far done. But, for many minutes, the heart beat on with a muffled sound. This, however, did not trouble me; it would not be heard through the wall. At length it stopped. The old man was dead. I removed the bed and examined the corpse. Yes, he was stone, stone dead. I placed my hand upon the heart and held it there many minutes. There was no pulse. He was stone dead. His eye would trouble me no more.

If still you think me mad, you will think so no longer when I describe the great care I took to hide the body. The night went by, and I worked quickly, but in silence. First of all I worked on the corpse. I cut off the head and the arms and the legs.

I then took up three boards from the floor of the bedroom, and put all underneath. I then put back the boards so cleverly, skillfully, that no human eye—not even *his*—could have noticed anything wrong. There was nothing to wash out—no stain of any kind—no blood-spot whatever. I had been too careful for that. A tub had caught all—ha! ha!

When I had finished, it was four o'clock—and still dark as midnight. As the bell sounded the hour, there came a knocking at the street door. I went down to open it with a light heart—for what had I *now* to fear? Three men entered who introduced themselves, with perfect politeness, as officers of the police. A loud shriek had been heard by a neighbor during the night; questions had been asked; information had been brought to the police office, and they (the officers) had been sent to search the house.

I smiled—for *what* had I to fear? I made the gentlemen welcome. That shriek, I said, was my own in a dream. The old man, I mentioned, was absent in the country. I took my visitors all over the house. I made them search—search *well.* I led them, at length, to *his* bedroom. I showed them his treasures, safe, undisturbed. In almost a happy mood, I brought chairs into the room, and asked them to rest *here* from their work, while I myself, in the wild joy of my perfect victory, placed my own seat upon the very spot under which lay the corpse of the victim.

The officers were satisfied. My *manner* had convinced them. I was completely at ease. They sat, and while I answered cheerily, they talked about familiar things. But, before long, I felt myself getting pale. I wished they were gone. My head ached, and I thought I heard a ringing in my ears; but still they sat and still talked. The ringing became more distinct—it continued and became more distinct: I talked more freely to get rid of the feeling: but it continued even more distinctly—until, at length, I found that the noise was *not* in my own head.

No doubt I now grew *very* pale—but I talked more rapidly, and with a louder voice. Yet the sound increased—and what could I do? It was *a low, dull, quick sound—much such a sound as a watch makes when surrounded by cotton.* I gasped for breath—and yet the officers heard it not. I talked more quickly—more excitedly; but the noise steadily increased. I stood up and argued about little things, in a high voice and with much waving of the arms, but the noise steadily increased. Why *would* they not be gone? I paced the floor to and fro with heavy steps—but the noise steadily increased. Oh God! what *could* I do? I shouted—I swore! I pushed the chair I had been sitting on noisily across the boards, but the sound underneath continually increased. It grew louder—louder—*louder!* And still the men talked pleasantly, and smiled. Was it possible they did not hear it? Almighty God! —no, no! They heard!—they suspected!—they *knew!*—they were making a joke of my horror!—this I thought, and this I think. But anything was better than this torture! Anything was better than the look in their eyes! I could bear those knowing smiles no longer! I felt that I must scream or die!—and now—again!—listen! louder! louder! louder! *louder!*—

"Villains!" I shrieked, "pretend no more! I admit the crime!—tear up the boards!—here, here!—it is the beating of his hideous heart!"

Recall

1. Throughout the story, the narrator (the person who tells the story) claims that he is not (a) a murderer (b) a madman (c) a careful person.
2. The narrator says he killed the old man (a) for his gold (b) because of his evil eye (c) because he hated him.

3. For a week before the crime, the narrator (a) tried to get someone else to kill the old man (b) tried not to commit murder (c) entered the old man's room at midnight.
4. The murder was committed on the eighth night because (a) the evil eye was open (b) the shades were finally drawn (c) the narrator had to leave town the following day.
5. For an hour before his murder, the old man (a) slept peacefully (b) sat in frightened silence (c) tried to leave the room.
6. The narrator kills his victim with a (a) bed (b) gun (c) rope.
7. The narrator first hears the beating of the heart (a) before the crime (b) as the murder takes place (c) several hours after the murder.
8. To hide the body, the narrator uses the skills of a (a) plumber (b) gravedigger (c) carpenter.
9. "A tub had caught all—ha! ha!" The word *all* refers to (a) laundry (b) water (c) blood.
10. The police officers came because (a) the narrator had called them (b) a shriek had been heard (c) light had been seen at the windows.
11. As the police first searched the house, the narrator claims he was (a) completely at ease (b) nervous (c) pale.
12. After the search, the narrator talks to the police officers (a) right over the dead man's body (b) in the cellar (c) outside the house.
13. Toward the end of the story, the narrator says that the noise he hears (a) gets softer and softer (b) gets louder and louder (c) disappears altogether.
14. When he confesses, the narrator seems sure that the police (a) do not suspect him (b) are about to leave (c) can hear the noise too.

Infer

15. The narrator does not know that he is very (a) clever (b) insane (c) careful.
16. The narrator (a) knows himself very well (b) knows only part of what is important (c) knows absolutely nothing about himself.
17. Actually, the police officers (a) don't hear the heart beating (b) hear the sound, but only softly (c) hear the sound as the narrator hears it.
18. An important subject not mentioned by the narrator is (a) murder (b) lanterns (c) guilt.
19. Which statement best sums up the story? (a) Madmen, who have no guilt feelings, can commit perfect crimes. (b) A killer's secret guilt may make him hear imaginary noises that force him to confess. (c) No matter how smart a criminal is, the police are smarter.
20. The story shows that the author, Edgar Allan Poe, (a) was a madman (b) had been mad at one time in his life (c) could write as a madman might write.

Vocabulary Review

1. The noise of a car's exhaust is usually *muffled* and not *distinct.* The words *muffled* and *distinct* could refer to (a) tires and engines (b) soft sounds and loud sounds (c) men and women.
2. The *vulture* ate the *victim* of the flood. The words *vulture* and *victim* could refer to (a) an alligator and a fish (b) a fox and a rabbit (c) a bird and a rabbit.

3. A *film* over a person's eye would probably (a) harm sight (b) help sight (c) have no effect on sight.
4. Something done by *instinct* is done (a) naturally (b) as part of a well-thought-out plan (c) under the direction of other people.
5. A *hideous villain* would probably be an (a) ugly farm worker (b) handsome farm worker (c) ugly criminal.

Critical Thinking

1. Much of "The Tell-Tale Heart" has meaning on two levels: the narrator says one thing; you, as a reader, are supposed to think something quite different. (a) In the first paragraph the narrator claims he is not mad. Look back at the story. When did you begin to think the narrator was mad? When were you sure? Why? (b) Also in the first paragraph, the narrator says he will tell his story "calmly." In reading the story, how did you know he was not calm? For instance, why does the author use all the dashes (—) and exclamation points (!)? (c) In the first paragraph too, the narrator boasts about his hearing. Where in the story is his hearing shown not to be so good as he believes?
2. Find one more place in the story where you, as a reader, are supposed to think just the opposite of what the narrator says.
3. Some readers think Edgar Allan Poe used too much horror in his stories. These readers object to things like the cutting up of the body. ("A tub had caught all—ha! ha!") But aside from the horror, is there any *other* reason the author might

have had the body cut up? Why is it absolutely necessary for you, as a reader, to know that the old man is "stone, stone dead"?

4. Most readers do not notice that the words *heart* and *beat* are not used from the time the police arrive until the very end of the story. Why do you think the author avoided them? What does their absence tell us about the narrator's state of mind?

5. "Guilt will out" is an old saying. In other words, you can't keep guilty feelings inside of you. In your experience, how true is the saying? Would you agree with this statement: *No one can be sure at the time he does something wrong that his guilt will not come out?* Explain.

The Water Ghost of Harrowby Hall

John Kendrick Bangs

What's the recipe for a good ghost story? John Kendrick Bangs knew it well: take one haunted house, add one troubled owner, blend in the ghost of someone who lived in the house years before, and cook up a plan to finally get rid of the ghost— forever. *In the story that follows, the house is Harrowby Hall, owned for years by the Oglethorpe family of England. The ghost is a watery young woman of haunting beauty. And as for the plan, read on . . . and learn just how bad it can be to have the chance of a ghost.*

Vocabulary Preview

ASBESTOS (as-BES-tus) building material that is fireproof
• The walls of the furnace room were lined with *asbestos.*

COLD STORAGE (KOLD STOR-ij) the keeping of food or goods in a place made cold, often by refrigeration
• Potatoes in *cold storage* will keep nearly a year.

DEWY (DOO-ee) covered with dew, or small drops of water
• The *dewy* grass sparkled in the early morning sunlight.

DIVING HELMET (DI-ving HEL-mut) the head covering used by deep-sea divers
• The *diving helmet* protects the diver's head and helps him to breathe.

GURGLING (GUR-gling) flowing or bubbling with a soft, uneven sound
• The *gurgling* water disappeared down the drain.

WAREHOUSE (WARE-house) a building where goods are stored, or kept safely
• The Smiths put their furniture in a *warehouse* when they went overseas.

THE TROUBLE WITH HARROWBY HALL WAS that it was haunted. And what was worse, the ghost was not satisfied with simply appearing at the bedside of the poor person who saw it. No, the ghost insisted on staying there for one whole hour before it would disappear.

It never appeared except on Christmas Eve, and then just as the clock was striking twelve. The owners of Harrowby Hall had done their best to get rid of the damp and dewy lady who rose up out of the floor of a guest bedroom at midnight, but with no luck. They had tried to stop the clock, so that the ghost would not know when it was midnight. But she had made her appearance just the same. She had stood there until everything around her was thoroughly soaked with water.

Then the owners of Harrowby Hall filled every crack in the floor with black tar, and over this placed layers of heavy cloth. The walls were made waterproof, and the doors and windows also. The owners hoped that the liquid lady would find it difficult to leak into a room which no water could enter. But even this did no good. The following Christmas Eve she appeared as easily as before. She frightened the guest in the room out of his senses by sitting down beside him and gazing with her deep blue eyes into his. In her long, bony fingers were bits of dripping seaweed, the ends hanging down. She drew these ends across the guest's forehead until he became like one insane. And then he fainted away, and was found in his bed the next morning, soaked with seawater and fright.

The next year the owner of Harrowby Hall decided not to have the best guest bedroom opened at all. He hoped that perhaps the ghost would be satisfied by haunting the furniture. But the plan was as useless as the many that had gone before it.

The ghost appeared as usual in the room—that is, it was supposed she did, for the curtains were dripping wet the next morning. Finding no one there, she immediately set out to learn the reason why. She chose to haunt none other than the owner of the Harrowby himself. She found him in his own room drinking whiskey and congratulating himself upon having fooled the water ghost. All of a sudden the curl went out of his hair, his whiskey bottle filled and overflowed, and he was himself dripping wet. When he had recovered from the shock, which was a painful one, he saw before him the lady with the deep blue eyes and the seaweed fingers. The sight was so unexpected and so terrifying that he fainted. But the huge amount of water in his hair, trickling down over his face, made him immediately come to.

Now it so happened that the owner of Harrowby was a brave old man. Although he did not particularly like talking to ghosts, especially such a liquid ghost as the one now before him, he was not to be stopped. He had paid the lady the compliment of fainting from his first surprise. And now that he had come to, he intended to find out a few things he felt he had a right to know. He would have liked to put on a dry suit of clothes first, but the ghost refused to leave him for an instant until her hour was up. Every time he would move she would follow him, with the result that everything she came near got a soaking. In an effort to warm himself up, he walked to the fireplace—a bad move as it turned out, because it brought the ghost too near the fire, which immediately went out. The only thing he could do for himself was to swallow two small cold pills, which he managed to put into his mouth before the ghost had time to interfere. Having done this, he turned quickly to the ghost, and said:

"Far be it from me to be impolite to a woman, madam. But I'm hanged if it wouldn't please me better if you'd stop these visits of yours to this house. Go sit out on the lake, if you like that sort of thing. Please do not, I beg you, come into a gentleman's house and soak him and his furniture in this way. It is disagreeable."

"Henry Hartwick Oglethorpe," said the ghost, in a gurgling voice, "you don't know what you're talking about."

"Madam," returned the unhappy man, "I only wish that remark were true. I was talking about you. It would be money—much money—in my pocket, madam, if I did not know you."

"That is a bit of silly nonsense," replied the ghost, throwing about a quart of sudden anger into the face of the owner. "You do not know that I am forced to haunt this place year after year by a fate I cannot escape. It is no pleasure to me to enter this house and ruin everything I touch. I never wanted to be a showerbath, but so it must be. Do you know who I am?"

"No, I don't," returned the owner of Harrowby. "The Lady of the Lake?"

"You're a funny man for your years," said the ghost. "Well, I have been doing this highly unpleasant job for two hundred years tonight."

"How the devil did you ever get started?" asked the owner.

"Through a suicide," replied the other. "I am the ghost of that fair young woman whose picture hangs over the fireplace in the living room. I should have been your great-great-great-great-great aunt if I had lived, Henry Hartwick Oglethorpe. You see, I was the sister of your great-great-great-great-grandfather."

"But what made you decide to haunt this house?"

"I was not to blame, sir," returned the lady. "It was my

father's fault. He it was who built Harrowby Hall, and the haunted bedroom was to have been mine. My father had it done up in pink and yellow, knowing well that blue and gray were the only two colors I could stand. He did it simply to anger me! And when I refused to live in the room, my father said I could live there or on the lawn, he didn't care which. That night I ran from the house and jumped over the cliff into the sea."

"That was unnecessary," said the owner of Harrowby.

"So I now know," returned the ghost. "If I had known what the results were to be, I would not have jumped. But I really never realized what I was doing until after I was drowned. I hadn't been drowned a week when a sea spirit came to me and said that I must haunt Harrowby Hall for one hour every Christmas Eve throughout the rest of time. I was to haunt that room on Christmas Eve if I found someone in it; and if not, I was to spend the hour with the head of the house."

"I'll sell the place."

"That you cannot do, for it is also required that I shall appear in front of anyone who might buy the house, and tell him the awful secret."

"Do you mean to tell me that every time I don't happen to have a guest in that room, you are going to haunt *me,* wherever I may be?" demanded the owner.

"You have spoken the truth, Oglethorpe. And what is more," said the water ghost, "it doesn't make the slightest difference where you are. If I find that room empty, wherever you may be I shall soak you with my——"

Here the clock struck one, and immediately the ghost faded away. It was perhaps more of a trickle than a fade, but it was a complete disappearance. And as for the owner of Harrowby, when Christmas Eve came again he was in his grave, never having gotten over the cold he caught that awful night. Harrowby Hall was now the property of the dead owner's son, who lived in London. That night in his bedroom he had the same experience that his father had gone through. But the son, being younger and stronger, survived the shock. Everything in his room was ruined. His clocks were rusted, and a fine collection of water-color paintings was ruined. What was worse, the apartment below his was soaked with water dripping through the floor. He had to pay for the damage, and his landlady asked that he leave the rooms immediately.

The story of the curse upon his family had become known, and no one would invite him anywhere in the evening. Fathers of daughters would not permit him to remain in their houses later than eight o'clock at night. Nor would the girls themselves have much to do with him, fearing the watery lady with whom, it was said, he held midnight meetings.

So the young owner of Harrowby Hall decided, as all the Oglethorpes before him had decided, that something must be done. His first thought was to make one of his servants sleep in the haunted room. But the servants knew the history of the room and refused. None of his friends would agree to sleep in the room, nor was there to be found in all England a person so poor as to stay in the haunted room on Christmas Eve for pay.

Then the new owner thought about having the fireplace in the room made bigger, so that he might dry up the ghost at its first appearance. But he remembered what his father had told him—that no fire could stand up to the lady's dampness.

It was then that the natural action of his mind, in going from one opposite to the other, suggested a plan. It was the way in which the water ghost was finally defeated, and happiness once more came to the house of Oglethorpe.

The owner found himself a warm suit of long underwear.

Putting this on, he placed over it a tight-fitting rubber suit. On top of this he placed another set of long underwear made of wool, and over this a second rubber suit like the first. Upon his head he placed a light and comfortable diving helmet. Dressed this way on the following Christmas Eve, he awaited the ghost's coming.

It was a bitterly cold night. The air outside was still, and the temperature was well below zero. Inside the quiet house the owner lay on the bed in the haunted room dressed as has already been described, and then——

The clock clanged out the hour of twelve.

There was a sudden banging of doors, a blast of cold air swept through the halls, the door leading into the haunted room flew open, a splash was heard, and the water ghost was seen standing at the side of the owner of Harrowby. His rubber suit was already streaming with water. But deep down under his clothing, he was as dry and as warm as he could have wished.

"Ha!" said the young owner of Harrowby. "I'm glad to see you."

"You are the most original man I've met, if that is true," returned the ghost. "May I ask, where *did* you get that hat?"

"Certainly, madam," returned the owner politely. "It's just a little nothing in the new style that I picked up for emergencies. But, tell me, is it true that you are going to follow me about for one whole hour—to stand where I stand, to sit where I sit?"

"That is my fate," returned the lady.

"We'll go out on the lake," said the owner, starting up.

"You can't get rid of me that way," returned the ghost. "The water won't swallow me up. In fact, it will just make me all the wetter."

"Nevertheless," said the owner firmly, "we will go out on the lake."

"But, my dear sir," returned the ghost, "it is very, very cold out there. You will be freezing before you've been out ten minutes."

"Oh, no, I'll not," replied the owner. "I am very warmly dressed. Come!" This last word was said in a tone of command that made the ghost ripple.

And they started.

They had not gone far before the water ghost showed signs of alarm.

"You walk too slowly," she said. "I am nearly frozen. My knees are so stiff now I can hardly move. I beg you to quicken your step."

"I should like to please a lady," returned the owner, "but my clothes are rather heavy, and a hundred yards an hour is about my speed. Indeed, I think we would better sit down here on this snowdrift, and talk matters over."

"Do not! Do not do so, I beg!" cried the ghost. "Let me move on. I feel myself growing stiff as it is. If we stop here, I shall be frozen."

"That, madam," said the owner slowly, seating himself on a cake of ice—"that is why I have brought you here. We have been outside just ten minutes; we have fifty more. Take your time about it madam, but freeze, that is all I ask of you."

"I cannot move my right leg now," cried the ghost, in despair. "And my skirt is a solid sheet of ice. Oh, good, kind Mr. Oglethorpe, light a fire, and let me go free from these icy chains."

"Never, madam. It cannot be. I have you at last."

"Alas!" cried the ghost, a tear freezing on her icy cheek. "Help me, I beg. I'm freezing!"

"Freeze, madam, freeze!" returned Oglethorpe coldly. "You have soaked me and my family for two hundred and three years, madam. Tonight you have had your last haunt."

"Ah, but I shall thaw out again, and then you'll see!" cried the lady. "Instead of the really good ghost I have been in my past, sir, I shall be icewater!"

"No, you won't, either," returned Oglethorpe. "For when you are frozen quite stiff, I shall send you to a cold-storage warehouse, and there you shall remain an icy work of art forever."

"But warehouses burn."

"So they do, but this warehouse cannot burn. It is made of asbestos and surrounding it are fireproof walls. Inside those walls the temperature shall forever be 416 degrees below zero; low enough to make an icicle of any flame in this world—or the next," the owner added, with a little laugh.

"For the last time let me beg of you. I would kneel to pray for your kindness, Oglethorpe, but my knees are already frozen. I beg of you do not doo——"

Here even the words froze on the water ghost's lips, and the clock struck one. There was a little quiver throughout the icy form. The moon, coming out from behind a cloud, shone down on the statue of a beautiful woman in clear, transparent ice. There stood the ghost of Harrowby Hall, defeated by the cold, a prisoner for all time.

The owner of Harrowby had won at last. And even today, in a strange warehouse in London, stands the frozen form of one who will never again flood the house of Oglethorpe with sorrow and seawater.

As for the owner of Harrowby, his success in dealing with the ghost has made him famous, although his victory took place some twenty years ago. And far from being unpopular, as he was when we first knew him, he has not only been married twice, but is to lead a third bride to the altar before the year is out.

Recall

1. The water ghost appears regularly on (a) the owner's birthday (b) Christmas Eve (c) Saturday.
2. The water ghost has (a) seaweed hair (b) seaweed in her fingers (c) a dress made of seaweed.
3. The first place visited by the ghost is always (a) the owner's bedroom (b) the servants' room (c) the best guest bedroom.
4. The ghost has haunted Harrowby Hall for about (a) ten years (b) a hundred years (c) two hundred years.
5. Early in the story, the water ghost explains that she (a) dislikes her job (b) likes her job (c) enjoys haunting only members of the Oglethorpe family.
6. The water ghost blames her past troubles on (a) her mother (b) her father (c) a jealous cousin.
7. The owner who first talks to the ghost—the brave whiskey drinker—(a) ends his life by suicide (b) is drowned by the water ghost (c) dies of a bad cold.
8. The next owner is a young man who finds that the ghost affects his (a) means of earning a living (b) popularity (c) health.
9. The new owner decides that the ghost can best be defeated by (a) heat (b) dryness (c) cold.
10. His final plan requires (a) special clothing (b) the help of the police (c) a large fireplace.
11. "May I ask, where *did* you get that hat?" The word *hat* refers to (a) a pillow (b) wool earmuffs (c) a diving helmet.

12. The water ghost obeys the command to go outside with the new owner because (a) she really wants to go to the lake (b) it is her fate to follow him about for one hour (c) she wants to end her existence as a ghost.
13. Toward the end of the story, the young man (a) remains deaf to the ghost's requests (b) weakens when he understands the ghost's true feelings (c) starts to fall in love with the ghost.
14. The special warehouse is necessary so that the ghost will never (a) burn (b) dry up (c) thaw out.
15. At the end of the story, the ghost is best described as (a) the owner's bride (b) an icy statue (c) an ugly prisoner.

Infer

16. The reason the ghost's eyes are *deep blue* is probably that (a) all ghosts have blue eyes (b) this is often the color of the sea (c) the color indicates her feelings.
17. It is not clear from the story whether or not Harrowby Hall (a) serves good food (b) legally belongs to the Oglethorpes (c) was ever the home of the girl who became the ghost.
18. According to the story, ghosts (a) can do anything they wish (b) really possess no supernatural powers (c) must sometimes behave in a certain way.
19. At the end of the story, the author probably wants you to (a) be overjoyed to see the ghost defeated (b) wish you were the ghost (c) feel a little sorry for the ghost.

20. "The Water Ghost of Harrowby Hall" is different from most other ghost stories because it (a) is meant to be taken seriously (b) is humorous in places (c) contains living people as well as ghosts.

Vocabulary Review

1. In a *cold storage warehouse,* you would be most likely to find (a) carrots and potatoes (b) ice cubes (c) very old newspapers.
2. The small *asbestos* mat that some cooks keep near the stove will never (a) get lost (b) be useful (c) burn.
3. If you walk through a lot of *dewy* grass, your shoes will certainly be (a) dusty (b) wet (c) burned.
4. You would be most likely to use a *diving helmet* to (a) meet a ghost (b) dive from a diving board (c) find undersea treasures.
5. *Gurgling* water is always (a) in motion (b) steaming (c) dirty.

Critical Thinking

1. The water ghost is certainly unlike the ghost in any other story. Think of three words that describe the water ghost's personality. Explain at least three ways the water ghost differs from your idea of a "ghost."

2. What were your feelings at the end of the story? Was your sympathy with the young man, the ghost, or halfway between? Explain why you felt as you did.

3. The author, John Kendrick Bangs, attempted to write a new kind of ghost story: one that was not scary but amusing. How well do you think he succeeded? If you were given the chance to rewrite the story, what changes would you make? Why?

August Heat

W. F. Harvey

Has the heat on a broiling summer day ever made you feel that the world was strangely unreal? that the impossible could almost happen? If so, the story that follows is just for you. "August Heat" is a masterpiece, a tale with a double twist that will tie your brain in knots of pure delight. It was written some years ago by an Englishman, and the vocabulary may cause a little trouble. But take the time to understand every word. The story is worth the effort.

Vocabulary Preview

CHISEL (CHIZ-ul) a sharp tool used to cut or shape wood, stone, or metal

• The carpenter used a *chisel* to cut a hole in the door for the lock.

FLAW (FLAW) a small crack or other weakness

• The sidewalk outside school contains many *flaws*.

IMPROBABLE (im-PROB-uh-bul) that which is not probable, or not likely to happen

• Marty wastes a lot of time worrying about the *improbable*.

MARBLE (MAR-bul) a kind of stone used in building

• Many old banks are built of *marble*.

OASIS (o-AY-sis) a place where water is found in a desert

• Camels can travel several days between one *oasis* and another.

SKETCH (SKECH) a drawing

• The artist made a quick *sketch* of my sister Lianne.

TOMBSTONE (TOOM-stone) a stone that marks a grave in a cemetery

• Some old people order their *tombstones* before they die.

PHENISTONE ROAD, CLAPHAM, AUGUST 20th, 19—. I have had what I believe to be the most remarkable day in my life, and while the events are still fresh in my mind, I wish to put them down on paper as clearly as possible.

Let me say at the outset that my name is James Clarence Withencroft.

I am forty years old, in perfect health, never having known a day's illness.

By profession I am an artist, not a very successful one, but I earn enough money by my black-and-white work to satisfy my necessary wants.

My only near relative, a sister, died five years ago, so that I am independent.

I breakfasted this morning at nine, and after glancing through the morning paper I lighted my pipe and proceeded to let my mind wander in the hope that I might chance upon some subject for my pencil.

The room, though door and windows were open, was oppressively[1] hot, and I had just made up my mind that the coolest and most comfortable place in the neighborhood would be the deep end of the public swimming pool, when the idea came.

I began to draw. So intent was I on my work that I left my lunch untouched, only stopping work when the clock of St. Jude's struck four.

The final result, for a hurried sketch, was, I felt sure, the best thing I had done.

[1]*oppressively* (uh-PRES-uv-lee)—harshly; very uncomfortably; in a way which is hard to bear.

It showed a criminal in the courtroom immediately after the judge had pronounced sentence. The man was fat—enormously fat. The flesh hung in rolls about his chin; it creased his huge, stumpy neck. He was clean shaven (perhaps I should say a few days before he must have been clean shaven) and almost bald. He stood in the courtroom, his short, clumsy fingers clasping the rail, looking straight in front of him. The feeling that his expression conveyed[2] was not so much one of horror as of utter, absolute[3] collapse.

There seemed nothing in the man strong enough to sustain[4] that mountain of flesh.

I rolled up the sketch, and without quite knowing why, placed it in my pocket. Then with the rare sense of happiness which the knowledge of a good thing well done gives, I left the house.

I believe that I set out with the idea of calling upon Trenton, for I remember walking along Lytton Street and turning to the right along Gilchrist Road at the bottom of the hill where the men were at work on the new streetcar lines.

From there onwards I have only the vaguest recollections of where I went. The one thing of which I was fully conscious was the awful heat, that came up from the dusty asphalt pavement as an almost solid wave. I longed for the thunder promised by the great banks of copper-colored cloud that hung low over the western sky.

I must have walked five or six miles, when a small boy roused me from my reverie[5] by asking the time.

It was twenty minutes to seven.

When he left me I began to take stock of my bearings. I found myself standing before a gate that led into a yard bordered by a strip of thirsty earth, where there were flow-

[2]*conveyed* (kun-VAYD)—communicated.
[3]*absolute* (AB-suh-loot)—complete; total.
[4]*sustain* (suh-STAYN)—hold up; support.
[5]*reverie* (REV-uh-ree)—daydream.

ers, purple stock and scarlet geranium. Above the entrance was a board with the inscription—

CHS. ATKINSON TOMBSTONES
WORKER IN ENGLISH AND ITALIAN MARBLES

From the yard itself came a cheery whistle, the noise of hammer blows, and the cold sound of steel meeting stone.

A sudden impulse made me enter.

A man was sitting with his back towards me, busy at work on a slab of curiously veined marble. He turned round as he heard my steps and stopped short.

It was the man I had been drawing, whose portrait lay in my pocket.

He sat there, huge and fat, the sweat pouring from his scalp, which he wiped with a red silk handkerchief. But though the face was the same, the expression was absolutely different.

He greeted me smiling, as if we were old friends, and shook my hand.

I apologized for my intrusion.[6]

"Everything is hot and glary outside," I said. "This seems an oasis in the wilderness."

"I don't know about the oasis," he replied, "but it certainly is hot, as hot as hell. Take a seat, sir!"

He pointed to the end of the gravestone on which he was at work, and I sat down.

"That's a beautiful piece of stone you've got hold of," I said.

He shook his head. "In a way it is," he answered; "the surface here is as fine as anything you could wish, but there's a big flaw at the back, though I don't expect you'd ever notice it. I could never make really a good job of a bit of marble like

[6]*intrusion* (in-TROO-zhun)—act of coming unasked or unwanted.

that. It would be all right in the summer like this; it wouldn't mind the blasted heat. But wait till the winter comes. There's nothing quite like frost to find out the weak points in stone."

"Then what's it for?" I asked.

The man burst out laughing.

"You'd hardly believe me if I was to tell you it's for an exhibition, but it's the truth. Artists have exhibitions: so do grocers and butchers; we have them too. All the latest little things in headstones, you know."

He went on to talk of marbles, which sort best withstood wind and rain, and which were easiest to work; then of his garden and a new sort of carnation he had bought. At the end of every other minute he would drop his tools, wipe his shining head, and curse the heat.

I said little, for I felt uneasy. There was something unnatural, uncanny,[7] in meeting this man.

I tried at first to persuade myself that I had seen him before, that his face, unknown to me, had found a place in some out-of-the-way corner of my memory, but I knew that I was doing little more than trying to fool myself.

Mr. Atkinson finished his work, spat on the ground, and got up with a sigh of relief.

"There! what do you think of that?" he said, with an air of evident pride.

The inscription which I read for the first time was this—

SACRED TO THE MEMORY
OF
JAMES CLARENCE WITHENCROFT.
BORN JAN. 18TH, 1860.
HE PASSED AWAY VERY SUDDENLY
ON AUGUST 20TH, 19—
"In the midst of life we are in death."

[7] *uncanny* (un-KAN-ee)—beyond the ordinary or normal; mysterious; uncomfortably strange.

For some time I sat in silence. Then a cold shudder ran down my spine. I asked him where he had seen the name.

"Oh, I didn't see it anywhere," replied Mr. Atkinson. "I wanted some name, and I put down the first that came into my head. Why do you want to know?"

"It's a strange coincidence, but it happens to be mine."

He gave a long, low whistle.

"And the dates?"

"I can only answer for one of them, and that's correct."

"It's a strange thing!" he said.

But he knew less than I did. I told him of my morning's work. I took the sketch from my pocket and showed it to him. As he looked, the expression of his face altered until it became more and more like that of the man I had drawn.

"And it was only the day before yesterday," he said, "that I told Maria there were no such things as ghosts!"

Neither of us had seen a ghost, but I knew what he meant.

"You probably heard my name," I said.

"And you must have seen me somewhere and have forgotten it! Were you at Clacton-on-Sea last July?"

I had never been to Clacton in my life. We were silent for some time. We were both looking at the same thing, the two dates on the gravestone, and one was right.

"Come inside and have some supper," said Mr. Atkinson.

His wife is a cheerful little woman, with the flaky red cheeks of the country-bred. Her husband introduced me as a friend of his who was an artist. The result was unfortunate, for after the sardines and watercress had been removed, she brought me out a Doré Bible,[8] and I had to sit and express my admiration for nearly half an hour.

[8]*Doré Bible*—a Bible illustrated by Paul Gustave Doré, a 19th century French painter and illustrator.

I went outside, and found Atkinson sitting on the gravestone smoking.

We resumed the conversation at the point we had left off.

"You must excuse my asking," I said, "but do you know of anything you've done for which you could be put on trial?"

He shook his head.

"I'm not a bankrupt, the business is prosperous enough. Three years ago I gave turkeys to some of the police at Christmas, but that's all I can think of. And they were small ones, too," he added as an afterthought.

He got up, fetched a can from the porch, and began to water the flowers. "Twice a day regular in the hot weather," he said, "and then the heat sometimes gets the better of the delicate ones. And ferns, good Lord! they could never stand it. Where do you live?"

I told him my address. It would take an hour's quick walk to get back home.

"It's like this," he said. "We'll look at the matter straight. If you go back home to-night, you take your chance of accidents. A cart may run over you, and there's always banana skins and orange peel, to say nothing of fallen ladders."

He spoke of the improbable with a seriousness that would have been laughable six hours before. But I did not laugh.

"The best thing we can do," he continued, "is for you to stay here till twelve o'clock. We'll go upstairs and smoke; it may be cooler inside."

To my surprise I agreed.

We are sitting in a long, low room beneath the roof. Atkinson has sent his wife to bed. He himself is busy sharpening some tools at a little oilstone, smoking one of my cigars the while.

The air seems charged with thunder. I am writing this at

a shaky table before the open window. The leg is cracked, and Atkinson, who seems a handy man with his tools, is going to mend it as soon as he has finished putting an edge on his chisel.

It is after eleven now. I shall be gone in less than an hour. But the heat is stifling.

It is enough to send a man mad.

Recall

1. The story starts with a date because (a) it is written in the form of a letter (b) W. F. Harvey started writing the story on that day (c) the date later turns out to be important.
2. On the first page of the story, Withencroft presents himself as being (a) a famous artist (b) quite an ordinary person (c) a man whose health has been seriously affected by the heat.
3. Withencroft's drawing shows a very fat man who has just (a) been interrupted at work (b) received a harsh sentence from a judge (c) finished making a tombstone.
4. Atkinson makes tombstones from (a) English and Italian marbles (b) pieces of black slate (c) concrete.
5. The first touch of horror for Withencroft comes when he sees (a) Atkinson (b) the tombstone (c) the tools Atkinson uses.
6. Atkinson put Withencroft's name on a tombstone (a) because he knew Withencroft would soon die (b) to play a joke on Withencroft (c) entirely by chance.

7. Atkinson states that the tombstone was made (a) for an exhibition (b) according to an order received by mail (c) to show a new way of lettering.
8. "I can only answer for one of them, and that's correct." The word *them* in this sentence refers to (a) names (b) places (c) dates.
9. One of Atkinson's hobbies is (a) attending trials (b) growing flowers (c) reading ghost stories.
10. Both Withencroft and Atkinson regard the mystery with (a) feelings of guilt (b) anger at one another (c) reasonable curiosity and worry.
11. At the end of the story, Atkinson is (a) working on a tombstone (b) watering flowers (c) sharpening a chisel.
12. The story happens (a) in about an hour (b) during one day (c) during most of two days.
13. In which order are the following objects mentioned in the story? (a) drawing, tombstone, chisel (b) tombstone, chisel, drawing (c) chisel, tombstone, drawing.
14. Which of the following events happens last? (a) Withencroft takes a walk (b) Atkinson finishes a tombstone (c) Atkinson invites Withencroft to supper.

Infer

15. Most of Withencroft's actions in the story seem to be (a) clearly understood by him (b) carried out to anger Atkinson (c) puzzling to Withencroft himself.
16. The author suggests that Withencroft's drawing shows Atkinson in the (a) past (b) present (c) future.

17. The author probably intended the story to (a) arouse a sense of horror (b) prove to the reader that ghosts exist (c) be very similar to events in his own life.
18. Atkinson invites Withencroft to stay till midnight (a) to protect him (b) because it's too hot to walk home (c) because he enjoys talking to Withencroft.
19. The author suggests that the most important event happened (a) before Withencroft started writing the story (b) during the story itself (c) after the writing ended.
20. This event was probably (a) a lonesome walk home (b) a murder (c) a thunderstorm.

Vocabulary Review

Below are *italicized* words from the story followed by sentences with blanks. On your paper, write the numeral of each sentence and the words that best fill the blanks. Use each word only once.

chisel	*improbable*	*oasis*	*tombstone*
flaw	*marble*	*sketch*	

1. The old blackboard had a(n)——— in one corner.
2. Donna always hopes for the ———, like getting an "A" in English.
3. The monument was made of huge blocks of ———.
4. Brad drew a(n) ——— of me yesterday.
5. Soft stone can be easily cut with a(n) ———.
6. The explorers finally found water at a(n) ———.
7. A small ——— was stolen from the cemetery.

Critical Thinking

1. The most important event in Withencroft's day is not included in the story. What is this event? Why isn't it part of the story he tells? Why *can't* it be?

2. Readers of the story differ from each other in getting the point. Some see what is going to happen as soon as Withencroft reads his name on the tombstone. Others catch on at the end. Still others never get the idea at all. Look back now at the story. What are the clues? Did you miss any the first time? Explain.

3. Most good stories contain an interesting series of events that could happen in real life. How true is this of "August Heat?" Why might "August Heat" be a good story only because it could *never* happen in real life?

4. The story seems very simple at first. Not until you finish reading it do you understand how skillfully it has been put together. How do any two of the following add to the story?

a) W. F. Harvey's simple, factual style of writing;
b) the mention of small details like times of day and names of streets;
c) Atkinson's interest in flowers;
d) the reason for Atkinson's invitation to stay till midnight;
e) the weather.

5. Sometimes the future does seem to be predicted by mysterious forces. Every so often we read strange stories in newspapers. For instance, a husband in New York dreams of an airplane crash. He telephones his wife, who is about to return from a visit to Chicago. She takes a train home—and sure enough, the plane she would otherwise have taken crashes. Describe an experience similar to this one that you have heard or read. Or make up a very short story that could really happen.

The Chaser

John Collier

To begin with, what is science fiction—*exactly? That's not an easy question. Some science-fiction stories are about monsters created by mad scientists, or little green men, or people whizzing through space in the year 3000. But others are about quite ordinary people. Many "sci-fi" stories ask* what would happen if *something now scientifically impossible were made possible:* What would happen if *the law of gravity could be canceled by pushing a button?* What would happen if *an "earthling" married a creature from Mars? The story you're about to read asks* what would happen if *a man could buy a drug that would turn any woman into the "perfect wife." Curious? Read on. . . .*

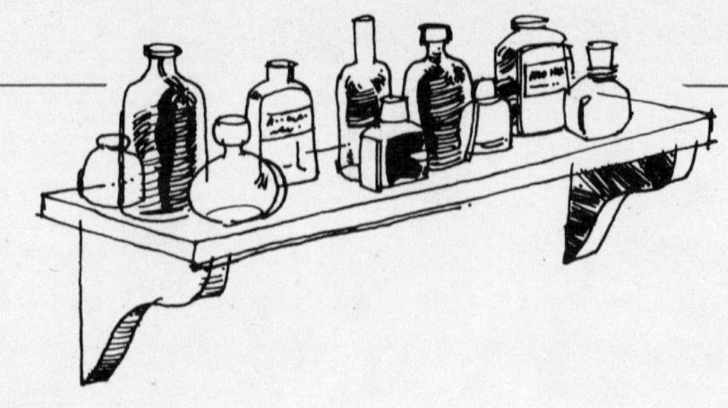

Vocabulary Preview

AU REVOIR (or-VWAR) French for "till we meet again"

- From the car window, Jeanette called, *"Au revoir."*

AUTOPSY (AW-top-see) an examination of a body to find the cause of death

- An *autopsy* showed Max had died of cancer.

CHASER (CHAY-sur) a lighter drink taken after hard liquor

- At the bar, the woman ordered whiskey and a beer *chaser.*

EFFECTIVE (ee-FEK-tiv) good for the purpose

- Marge found an *effective* cough medicine that really worked.

POTION (PO-shun) a liquid medicine or magic drug

- One spoonful of the *potion* put her to sleep.

ALAN AUSTEN, AS NERVOUS AS A KITTEN, went up certain dark and creaky stairs in the neighborhood of Pell Street, and peered about for a long time in the dim light before he found the name he wanted written on one of the doors.

He pushed open this door, as he had been told to do, and found himself in a tiny room, which contained no furniture but a plain kitchen table, a rocking-chair and an ordinary chair. On one of the dirty walls were a couple of shelves, containing in all perhaps a dozen bottles and jars.

An old man sat in the rocking-chair, reading a newspaper. Alan, without a word, handed him the card he had been given. "Sit down, Mr. Austen," said the old man very politely. "I am glad to make your acquaintance."

"Is it true," asked Alan, "that you have a certain mixture that has—er—quite unusual effects?"

"My dear sir," replied the old man, "my stock is not very large, but such as it is, it is excellent. I think nothing I sell has effects which could be described as usual."

"Well, the fact is—" began Alan.

"Here, for example," interrupted the old man, reaching for a bottle from the shelf. "Here is a liquid as colorless as water, almost tasteless, quite impossible to discover in coffee, milk, wine, or any other beverage. It is also quite impossible to discover by any known method of autopsy."

"Do you mean it is a poison?" cried Alan, very much horrified.

"Call it a glove-cleaner if you like," said the old man. "Maybe it will clean gloves. I have never tried. One might call it a life-cleaner. Lives need cleaning sometimes."

"I want nothing of that sort," said Alan.

"Probably it is just as well," said the old man. "Do you know the price of this? For one teaspoonful, which is enough, I ask five thousand dollars. Never less. Not a penny less."

"I hope all your mixtures are not as expensive," said Alan.

"Oh dear, no," said the old man. "It would be no good charging that sort of price for a love potion, for example. Young people who need a love potion very seldom have five thousand dollars. Otherwise they would not need a love potion."

"I am glad to hear that," said Alan.

"I look at it like this," said the old man. "Please a customer with one article, and he will come back when he needs another. Even if it *is* more costly. He will save up for it, if necessary."

"So," said Alan, "you really do sell love potions?"

"If I did not sell love potions," said the old man, reaching for another bottle, "I should not have mentioned the other matter to you. It is only when one is in a position to help that one can afford to be so honest."

"And these potions," said Alan. "They are not just—just —er—"

"Oh no," said the old man. "Their effects are permanent, and extend far beyond the first loving look. But they include it. Now—and forever."

"Dear me!" said Alan. "How very interesting!"

"But consider the serious side," said the old man.

"I do, indeed," said Alan.

"For coolness," said the old man, "they substitute real love. Give one tiny bit of this to the young lady—its flavor can't be noticed in orange juice, soup, or cocktails—and however foolish she is, she will change altogether. She will want nothing but to be alone with you."

"I can hardly believe it," said Alan. "She is so fond of parties."

"She will not like them any more," said the old man. "She will be afraid of the pretty girls you may meet."

"She will actually be jealous?" cried Alan in delight. "Of me?"

"Yes, she will want to be everything to you."

"She is, already. Only she doesn't care about it."

"She will, when she has taken this. She will really care. You will be her only interest in life."

"Wonderful!" cried Alan.

"She will want to know all you do," said the old man. "All that has happened to you during the day. Every word of it. She will want to know what you are thinking about, why you smile suddenly, why you are looking sad."

"That is love!" cried Alan.

"Yes," said the old man. "How carefully she will look after you! She will never allow you to be tired, to sit in a draught, to neglect your food. If you are an hour late, she will be terrified. She will think you are killed, or that some other woman has caught you."

"I can hardly imagine Diana like that!" cried Alan, overcome with joy.

"You will not have to use your imagination," said the old man. "And, by the way, since there are always other women, if by any chance you *should,* later on, slip a little, you need not worry. She will forgive you, in the end. She will be terribly hurt, of course, but she will forgive you—in the end."

"That will not happen," said Alan.

"Of course not," said the old man. "But, if it did, you need not worry. She would never divorce you. Oh, no! And, of course, she herself will never give you the least, the very least, reason to worry."

"And how much," said Alan, "is this wonderful mixture?"

"It is not as expensive," said the old man, "as the glove-cleaner, or life-cleaner, as I sometimes call it. No. That is five thousand dollars, never a penny less. One has to be older than you are, to buy that sort of thing. One has to save up for it."

"But the love potion?" said Alan.

"Oh, that," said the old man, opening the drawer in the kitchen table, and taking out a tiny, rather dirty-looking bottle. "That is just a dollar."

"I can't tell you how grateful I am," said Alan, watching him fill it.

"I like to help," said the old man. "Then customers come back, later in life, when they are rather more rich, and want more expensive things. Here you are. You will find it very effective."

"Thank you again," said Alan. "Good-by."

"Au revoir," said the old man.

Recall

1. The old man's place of business is (a) easy to find (b) hard to find (c) impossible to find.
2. The old man and Alan discuss (a) one drug (b) two drugs (c) three drugs.
3. The old man's "life-cleaner" is actually a (a) glove cleaner (b) love potion (c) poison.
4. Alan expresses great interest in the (a) glove cleaner (b) love potion (c) poison.
5. According to the old man, the effects of the love potion last (a) a few minutes (b) a few days (c) forever.
6. Alan intends to give the love potion to (a) Diana (b) the "other women" spoken of (c) himself.
7. Compared to the "life-cleaner," the love potion costs (a) much more (b) about the same (c) much less.

Infer

8. Throughout the story, Alan (a) is trying to fool the old man (b) understands what the old man is up to (c) does not understand the old man's plan.
9. At the end of the story, the old man expects Alan to come back to buy (a) a poison (b) more of the love potion (c) a cleaner for gloves.
10. Which sentence best expresses the main idea of the story? (a) True happiness is possible only with drugs. (b) A "dream wife" or "dream husband" would in fact be impossible to live with. (c) A good salesperson knows his customers well.

Vocabulary Review

1. The *chaser* in the story's title turns out to be (a) beer (b) poison (c) a love potion.
2. An *autopsy* in future years would most probably be performed on (a) Alan (b) Diana (c) the "other woman."
3. The old man tells Alan *"au revoir"* because he thinks Alan (a) will come back (b) will send Diana back (c) will lead a very happy life.
4. An *effective potion* is the same thing as (a) a good bottle of pills (b) an expensive drug (c) a good liquid drug.

Critical Thinking

1. Some readers finish the story believing that Alan will kill himself in future years. Find a sentence on page 99 that indicates this is not so. Explain.

2. Some other readers finish the story believing that Diana is a girl friend that Alan will never marry. Find a sentence on page 101 that indicates this is not so. Explain.

3. If you had only three words to describe Alan, what would they be? What would your three words for the old man be? Think of the characters' experience, intelligence, and outlook on life.

4. Explain in your own words what Alan does not understand about the person Diana will become after drinking the potion. What would be wrong with marriage to such a person?

5. Suppose the story happened in reverse, with Diana coming to the old man to buy a love potion for Alan. What might the old man say about the person Alan would become? Think of five qualities of the "perfect husband."

The New Accelerator

H. G. Wells

What would happen if . . . *a certain drug could turn a woman into the "perfect wife"? If you read the last story, you should have a pretty good idea. Now here's a new one:* What would happen if . . . *another drug could speed up the pace of life, so that you could do the work of an hour in a half-hour's time? You'd be able to do more, certainly. And you'd save a lot of time. But what else would happen? And what if time could be speeded up a thousand times? Or several thousand? In "The New Accelerator" these questions are dealt with by H. G. Wells (1866-1946), an important pioneer in science-fiction writing.*

Vocabulary Preview

ACCELERATOR (ak-SEL-uh-ray-tur) any device or substance that makes something go faster or quickens movement
• Trina pushed down on the *accelerator* pedal to make the car go faster.
• Chemical *accelerators* can make photographs develop faster.

BAY WINDOW (BAY WIN-doe) a large window or set of windows built to jut out from the side of a house or building
• The McAffees have a *bay window* in their living room.

FRICTION (FRIK-shun) the rubbing of one thing against another, producing heat
• You can feel the heat of *friction* if you rub your hands together hard.

PARASOL (PAIR-uh-sol) a kind of umbrella used to protect one from the sun's rays
• Years ago many women walked under *parasols* because sun tans were not thought to be attractive.

REALITY (ree-AL-uh-tee) a real thing or fact
• Space travel, once a dream, is now a *reality*.

VISIBLE (VIZ-uh-bul) able to be seen
• I heard the airplane, but because of the thick fog, it was not *visible*.

WINCED (WINST) pulled back in pain or fright
• Little Tommy *winced* when the big balloon popped.

CERTAINLY, IF EVER A MAN FOUND A diamond when he was looking for a dime, it is my good friend Professor Gibberne. I have heard before of scientists who surprised even themselves, but never quite as much as he has done. He has really found something to change human life completely. And he did this when he was simply looking for an all-around drug to bring tired people up to the demands of these busy days. I have tasted the stuff now several times, and I cannot do better than describe the effect it had on me.

Professor Gibberne, as many people know, is my neighbor. He lives in one of those pleasant little houses that make the western end of the Upper Sandgate Road so interesting. It is in the little room with the bay window that he works when he is in town, and in which we have so often smoked and talked together. He likes to talk to me about his work. He is one of those men who find a help in talking, and so I have been able to follow the New Accelerator right up from a very early state. Of course, most of his experiments are not done there, but in Gower Street, London, in a fine new laboratory next to the hospital.

As nearly everyone knows, Gibberne has gained much fame for his discoveries concerning the action of drugs upon the nervous system. We have him to thank for at least three absolutely safe drugs of unequaled value. "But none of these little things begin to satisfy me yet," he told me nearly a year ago. "Either they send a person up, or they send him down for a brief time. But what I want—and what I mean to have—is a drug that works all round, that wakes you up for a time from the top of your head to the tip of your big toe, and makes you go two—or even three to everybody else's one. Eh? That's the thing I'm after."

"It would tire a man," I said.

"Not a doubt of it. And you'd eat double or triple—and all that. But just think what the thing would mean. Imagine yourself with a little bottle like this"—he held up a little bottle of green glass—"and in it is the power to think twice as fast, move twice as quickly, do twice as much work in a certain time as you could otherwise do."

"But is such a thing possible?"

"I believe so. If it isn't, I've wasted my time for a year. Even if it was only one and a half times as fast, it would do."

"It *would* do!" I said.

"If you were a busy politician, for example, with time rushing up against you, something important to be done, eh? A person like that could gain—double time. And think if *you,* for example, wanted to finish a book."

"Usually," I said, "I wish I'd never begun them."

"Or a doctor worked to death, wants to sit down and think out a case. Or a lawyer—or a student cramming for an examination."

"Or in sports," I echoed.

"You see," said Gibberne, "if I get this all-round thing it will really do you no harm at all—except perhaps to the small degree it brings you nearer old age. You will just have lived twice to other people's once——"

"And you really think such a thing *is* possible?" I said.

"As possible," said Gibberne, and looked at something that went noisily by the window, "as a bus. As a matter of fact——"

He stopped and smiled at me deeply, and tapped slowly on the edge of his desk with the green bottle. "I think I know the secret. . . . Already I've got something coming." The nervous smile upon his face showed how serious he was. He rarely talked of his actual experiments unless things were very near the end. "And it may be, it may be—I shouldn't be surprised—it may even do the thing at a greater rate than twice."

"It will be a really big thing," I said.

"It will be, I think, a really big thing."

But I don't think he quite knew what a big thing it was to be, for all that.

I remember we had several talks about the stuff after that. "The New Accelerator" he called it. Sometimes he talked nervously of how it might make a lot of money. "It's a good thing," said Gibberne, "a tremendous thing. I know I'm giving the world something, and I think it only fair we should expect the world to pay."

My own interest in the coming drug certainly did not lessen. It seemed to me that Gibberne's drug was nothing less than amazing. Suppose a person took the drug often: he would live an active life indeed, but he would be an adult at eleven, middle-aged at twenty-five, and by thirty well on the road to old age. It was the 7th or 8th of August when he told me that the final experiment was going on as we talked, and it was on the 10th that he told me the thing was done. The New Accelerator was a reality. I met him as I was going up the Sandgate Hill—I think I was going to get my hair cut. He came hurrying down to meet me—I suppose he was coming to my house to tell me at once of his success. I remember that his eyes were unusually bright, and I noted even the swift bounce of his step.

"It's done," he cried, and gripped my hand, speaking very fast. "It's more than done. Come up to my house and see."

"Really?"

"Really!" he shouted. "Come up and see."

"And it does—twice?"

"It does more, much more. It scares me. Come up and

see the stuff. Taste it! Try it! It's the most amazing stuff on earth." He gripped my arm and, walking at a very fast pace, went shouting with me up the hill. It was one of those hot, clear days, with every color very bright. There was a breeze, of course, but not enough of a breeze to keep me cool and dry. I panted for mercy.

"I'm not walking fast, am I?" cried Gibberne, and slowed down to a quick march.

"You've been taking some of this stuff," I puffed.

"No," he said. "At the most, a drop of water that stood in a glass from which I had washed out the last of the stuff. I took some last night, you know. But that is history now."

"And it goes twice?" I said, nearing his doorway.

"It goes a thousand times, many thousand times!" cried Gibberne, flinging open the wooden gate to his small yard.

"Phew!" said I, and followed him to the door.

"I don't know how many times it goes," he said, with his key in his hand.

"And you ——"

"Heaven knows how many thousand times. The thing is to try the stuff now."

"Try the stuff?" I said, as we went along the hall.

"Yes," said Gibberne, turning on me in his study. "There it is in that little green bottle there! Unless you happen to be afraid?"

I am a careful man by nature. I *was* afraid. But on the other hand there is pride.

"Well," I stalled. "You say you've tried it?"

"I've tried it," he said, "and I don't look hurt by it, do I? And I *feel*——"

I sat down. "Give me the potion," I said. "If worst comes to worst, it will save having my hair cut. How do you take the mixture?"

"With water," said Gibberne, putting down a pitcher.

I made a gesture with my hand.

"I must warn you. As soon as you've got it down, shut your eyes, and open them very slowly in a minute or so. You'll still see. But there's a kind of shock if the eyes are open. Keep 'em shut."

"Shut," I said. "Good!"

"And the next thing is, keep still. Don't begin to move about. You may get a nasty bang if you do. Remember you will be going several thousand times faster than you ever did before, heart, lungs, muscles, brain—everything. But you won't know it. You'll feel just as you do now. Only everything in the world will seem to be going ever so many thousand times slower that it ever went before. That's what makes it so strange."

"Lord," I said. "And you mean——"

"You'll see," said he, and took up a little spoon. He glanced at the things on his desk. "Glasses," he said, "water. All here. Mustn't take too much the first time."

The little bottle glucked out its contents. "Don't forget what I told you," he said, turning the contents of the spoon into a glass. "Sit with the eyes tightly shut and in stillness for two minutes," he said. "Then you will hear me speak."

He added an inch or so of water to the little dose in each glass.

"By the way," he said, "don't put your glass down. Keep it in your hand and rest your hand on your knee. Yes—so. And now——"

He raised his glass.

"To the New Accelerator," I said.

"To the New Accelerator," he answered. We touched glasses and drank, and instantly I closed my eyes.

You know that blank feeling you get when you think

you're going to faint. For a time it was like that. Then I heard Gibberne telling me to wake up, and I opened my eyes. There he stood as he had been standing, glass still in hand. It was empty, that was all the difference.

"Well?" said I.

"Nothing wrong?"

"Nothing. A slight feeling of lightness, perhaps. Nothing more."

"Sounds?"

"Things are still," I said. "Yes! They *are* still. Except a sort of faint pat, patter, like rain falling on different things. What is it?"

"Slowed down sounds," I think he said, but I am not sure. He glanced at the window. "Have you ever seen a window curtain fixed in that way before?"

I followed his eyes, and there was the end of the curtain, frozen and stiff, corner high, in the act of flapping in the breeze.

"No," I said; "that's odd."

"And here," he said, and opened the hand that held the glass. Naturally I winced, expecting the glass to drop and smash. But it seemed to hang in mid-air—motionless. "Roughly speaking," said Gibberne, "an object falls 16 feet in the first second. This glass is falling 16 feet in a second now. Only, you see, it hasn't been falling yet for the hundredth part of a second. That gives you some idea of the speed of my Accelerator." And he waved his hand round and round, over and under the slowly sinking glass. Finally he took it by the bottom, pulled it down, and placed it very carefully on the table. "Eh?" he said to me, and laughed.

"That seems all right," I said, and began very carefully to raise myself from my chair. I felt perfectly well, very light and comfortable. I was going fast all over. My heart, for example, was beating a thousand times a second, but that caused me no pain at all. I looked out of the window. A motionless girl on a bicycle, head down and with a frozen puff of dust behind her rear wheel, tried to pass a slow truck that seemed not to move. "Gibberne," I cried, "how long will this amazing stuff last?"

"Heaven knows!" he answered. "Last time I took it I went to bed and slept it off. I tell you, I was frightened. It must have lasted some minutes, I think—it seemed like hours. But after a bit it slows down rather suddenly, I believe."

I was proud to notice that I did not feel frightened—I suppose because there were two of us. "Why shouldn't we go out?" I asked.

"Why not?"

"They'll see us."

"Not they. Goodness, no! Why, we shall be going a thousand times faster than the quickest card trick that was ever done. Come along! Which way shall we go? Window, or door?"

And out by the window we went.

I have had several strange experiences in my life, and imagined or read of others. But that little trip I made with Gibberne around town, under the influence of the New Accelerator, was the strangest and maddest of all. We went out by his gate into the road, and there we stopped to examine the people. There they were, people like ourselves and yet not like ourselves, frozen in careless movements. A girl and a boy smiled at one another, a smile that threatened to last forever. A woman rested her arm on the fence and stared at Gibberne's house with the endless stare of the dead. A man stretched a stiff hand with long fingers towards his loosened hat. We stared at them, we laughed at them, and we made faces at them. And then, a sort of disgust of them came upon us, and we turned away and walked towards the park.

"Goodness!" cried Gibberne, suddenly; "look there!"

He pointed, and there at the tip of his finger and sliding down the air with wings flapping slowly—was a bee.

The park seemed madder than ever. The band was playing in the stand, though all the sound it made for us was a low rattle. The music was a sort of last sigh that passed at times into a sound like the slow ticking of some huge clock. Frozen people stood silently, like dummies hung in mid-air. I passed close to a little poodle dog frozen in the act of jumping, and watched the slow movement of his legs as he sank to the earth. "Lord, look *here*!" cried Gibberne, and we halted for a moment. A tall person in white striped pants, white shoes, and a straw hat, had turned back to wink at two gaily dressed ladies he had passed. A wink, studied with slow care, is not a pleasant thing. It loses its happy quickness, and one notices that the winking eye does not completely close. Under its drooping lid appears the lower edge of an eyeball and a little line of white. "Heaven give me memory," said I, "and I will never wink again."

"Or smile," said Gibberne, with his eye on the lady's answering teeth.

"It's very hot, somehow," said I. "Let's go slower."

"Oh, come along!" said Gibberne.

We picked our way among the folding chairs in the path. Many of the people sitting in the chairs seemed almost natural. A purple-faced little gentleman was frozen trying to fold his newspaper against the wind, a breeze that we could not feel. We walked a little way from the crowd, and turned back to look at it. To see all those people, looking like figures of wax, was impossibly wonderful. Consider the wonder of it! All that I had said, and thought, and done since the stuff had begun to work on me, had happened, so far as those people went, in the twinkling of an eye. "The New Accelerator——" I began, but Gibberne interrupted me.

"There's that terrible old woman!" he said.

"What old woman?"

"Lives next door to me," said Gibberne. "Has a dog that barks. Gods! The temptation is strong!"

There is something like a boy about Gibberne at times. Before I could argue with him, he had dashed forward. He snatched the animal out of visible existence, and was running with it towards the cliff in the park. "Gibberne," I cried, "put it down!" Then I said something else. "If you run like that, Gibberne," I cried, "you'll set your clothes on fire. Your pants are going brown as it is!"

He put his hand on his leg and stood on the cliff's edge. "Gibberne," I cried, coming up, "put it down. This heat is too much! It's our running so! Two or three miles a second! Friction of the air!"

"What?" he said, glancing at the dog.

"Friction of the air," I shouted. "Friction of the air. Going too fast. Like shooting stars. Too hot. And, Gibberne! Gibberne! Look! You can see people moving slightly. I believe the stuff's working off! Put that dog down."

"Eh?" he said.

"It's working off," I repeated. "We're too hot and the stuff's working off! I'm wet through."

He stared at me, then at the band. The rattle of the instruments was certainly going faster. Then with a great sweep of the arm he threw the dog away from him. It went spinning upward, still frozen, and hung at last over the parasols of a group of talking people. Gibberne was holding my elbow. "Yes!" he cried. "I believe it is! That man's moving his handkerchief! I can see it. We must get out of this—now."

But we could not get out of it quickly enough. Luckily, perhaps! For we might have run, and if we had run, we might have burst into flames. Almost certainly we should have burst into flames! Neither of us had thought of that. . . . But before we could even begin to run, the effect of the drug had stopped. It was done in a fraction of a second. The effect of the New Accelerator vanished in the movement of a hand. I heard Gibberne's voice in alarm. "Sit down," he said, and flop, down I sat. As I did so, the slow noises of the band rushed together in a blast of music, and the people put their feet down and walked their ways. Papers and flags began flapping, smiles passed into words, the winking man finished his wink and went on his way, and all the seated people moved and spoke.

The whole world had come alive again, was going as fast as we were. Or rather, we were going no faster than the rest of the world. And the little dog, which had seemed to hang for a moment in the air, fell with a loud crash right through a lady's parasol!

That was what saved us. I doubt if a single person saw us suddenly become visible among them. Everyone was looking at the dog that had suddenly fallen through the parasol of a lady—in a slightly burned condition due to the high speed of its movements through the air. People got up and stepped on other people, and chairs were overturned. What happened then I do not know—we were much too anxious to get away from the affair. As soon as we were cool enough and had recovered from our confusion of mind, we stood up. Then, avoiding the crowd, we directed our steps back along the road below the park towards Gibberne's house.

So it was I had my first experience of the New Accelerator. We had been running about and doing all sorts of things in the space of a second or so of time. We had lived half an hour while the band had played, perhaps, two notes. But the effect it had upon us was that the whole world had stopped for our inspection.

Since that adventure, Gibberne has been steadily bringing the New Accelerator under control. I have several times taken it at his direction, without the slightest bad result. I may mention, for example, that with its help this story has been written at one sitting and without a stop, except for the nibbling of some chocolate. I began at 6:25, and by my watch it is now nearly 6:30. In the next few months, the discovery will be sold in all drug stores, in small green bottles. The price will be high but, considering its qualities, by no means impossible. Gibberne's Nervous Accelerator it will be called, and he hopes to be able to supply it in three strengths: one in 200, one in 900, and one in 2000, with yellow, pink, and white labels respectively. We shall see.

Recall

1. The narrator (the person who tells the story) knows Professor Gibberne because (a) they are both scientists (b) he is Gibberne's lawyer (c) they are neighbors.
2. Gibberne has become famous for discovering drugs that greatly affect (a) the nervous system (b) the heart (c) the leg and arm muscles.
3. At first, Gibberne expects the accelerator he's working on to speed things up (a) about twice (b) a thousand times (c) several thousand times.
4. One of Gibberne's plans for his discovery is to (a) give it to humanity (b) give it only to doctors (c) sell it and make money.
5. The first person to take the New Accelerator is (a) the narrator (b) Gibberne (c) a neighbor.
6. The narrator takes the New Accelerator (a) alone (b) with Gibberne (c) with a number of people in the park.
7. The New Accelerator speeds things up (a) about twice (b) a thousand times (c) several thousand times.

8. The first object that surprises the narrator after he's taken the New Accelerator is a (a) bicycle (b) bee (c) curtain.
9. To a person who has taken the New Accelerator, the rest of the world seems (a) speeded up (b) slowed down (c) about the same.
10. To the rest of the world, a person who has taken the New Accelerator is (a) clearly visible (b) seen only as a blur (c) not visible.
11. A word used several times to describe people on the street and in the park is (a) *cold* (b) *frozen* (c) *blue.*
12. Both Gibberne and the narrator forgot about (a) the accelerator's wearing off (b) the danger of bumping things (c) the heat produced by friction of the air.
13. No one notices the sudden appearance of the two men because of a (a) falling dog (b) flying cat (c) band concert.
14. According to the narrator, the story was written in about (a) five minutes (b) six hours (c) a week.
15. Gibberne's experiments with the accelerator make him decide to (a) keep it a secret (b) go ahead with his plans to sell it (c) give the formula only to the government.

Infer

16. If a person in the park had noticed the two men as they started to become visible, they would probably have seemed to be moving (a) quite fast (b) quite slowly (c) not at all.
17. The word that best describes Professor Gibberne is (a) *insane* (b) *ordinary* (c) *enthusiastic.*

18. The author's purpose in writing the story probably was to (a) describe something that will be possible in a few years (b) entertain through science fiction (c) tell the real life experience of its author, H. G. Wells.
19. Except for the New Accelerator itself, most other things in the story seem (a) possible (b) impossible (c) very doubtful.
20. One word in the story can't be found in the dictionary: "The little bottle *glucked* out its contents." The verb *gluck* probably refers to (a) sight (b) taste (c) sound.

Vocabulary Review

1. If you want to slow down a car, use the *brake;* if you want to speed up, use the (a) clutch (b) windshield (c) accelerator.
2. A *bay window* is a window that (a) looks out on a bay (b) looks like a fat person's stomach (c) sticks out from the side of a building.
3. If a friend *winced visibly* when something cold touched a bad tooth, he (a) hid his pain (b) pulled back in pain so that you could notice (c) asked you to look in his mouth.
4. If a person starts a fire by rubbing two sticks together, he's using (a) friction (b) fiction (c) fractions.
5. In H. G. Wells' story, the New Accelerator becomes a *reality* (a) on the first page (b) toward the middle (c) on the last page.
6. An *umbrella* is to *rain* as a *parasol* is to (a) *dust* (b) *snow* (c) *sunlight.*

Critical Thinking

1. Although an *accelerator* speeds things up, much of the story describes things that are slowed down. Explain in your own words how this is possible.

2. "I know I'm giving the world something," Professor Gibberne says early in the story, "and I think it only fair that we should expect the world to pay." Do you agree that people should be expected to pay high prices for new "wonder drugs"? Should such drugs belong to humanity or to the individuals (or companies) that discovered them? Explain your thinking.

3. Although today there is no drug which speeds things up thousands of times, one class of drugs, called *amphetamines* (am-FET-uh-meenz) does stimulate a person's heart and other organs to work faster. What are some harmful effects of amphetamines? What are some harmful effects of the New Accelerator mentioned by Wells in the story? What might be some harmful effects of a drug like the New Accelerator which the author never considered when writing the story?

4. In your opinion, if the New Accelerator became a reality tomorrow, would it be a new "wonder drug" or a dangerous, harmful drug? Explain.

Dr. Heidegger's Experiment

Nathaniel Hawthorne

There's really nothing new about science fiction. Remember the story about Ponce de Leon and the Fountain of Youth? In real life, Ponce de Leon was a Spanish explorer who conquered Puerto Rico and discovered Florida. In the science fiction of the time, Ponce de León was a Spanish explorer who wasted years searching Florida for a fountain whose water was supposed to make an old person young again. "Dr. Heidegger's Experiment" is a story about water from the Fountain of Youth. It was written by Nathaniel Hawthorne, an American author who lived from 1804 to 1864. You may find the writing a bit old-fashioned, but the story's idea is as new as your next thought. And "Dr. Heidegger's Experiment" will give you plenty to think about!

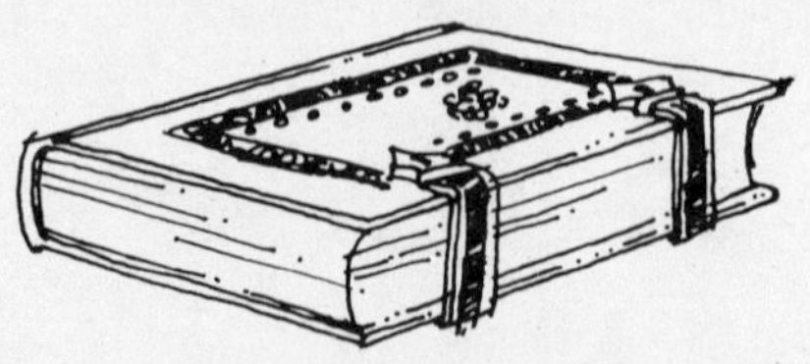

Vocabulary Preview

CLASP (KLASP) a clip or fastener
- Four metal *clasps* fastened the rack to the top of the car.

CRUMBLE (KRUM-bul) to fall into many small pieces
- Cake begins to *crumble* when it gets old and dry.

MAGNOLIA (mag-NO-lee-uh) a kind of flowering tree or bush
- The Wrights planted a *magnolia* in their front yard.

MELANCHOLY (MEL-un-kol-ee) gloomy; very sad and thoughtful
- Luis became *melancholy* when he couldn't find a job.

POLAR (PO-lur) of the North or South Pole
- Do *polar* bears live near the North or the South Pole?

PRIME (PRIME) the best part of something
- What age do you consider the *prime* of life?

WITHERED (WITH-urd) dried up, wrinkled and faded
- Old Mr. Tobias had a *withered* face.

THAT VERY STRANGE MAN, OLD Dr. Heidegger, once invited four old friends to meet him in his study. Three were white-bearded gentlemen, a Mr. Medbourne, a Colonel Killigrew, and a Mr. Gascoigne. The fourth was a wrinkled old lady, whose name was the Widow Wycherly. They were all melancholy old people who had been unfortunate in life. Mr. Medbourne, at one time, had been a rich businessman, but had lost everything through his greed. Colonel Killigrew had wasted his best years, and his health and money, in running after sinful pleasures. Mr. Gascoigne was a ruined politician, a man of evil fame. As for the Widow Wycherly, who had been a great beauty in her day, she now lived alone on account of certain stories which had prejudiced the people of the town against her. It is worth mentioning that each of these three old gentlemen, Mr. Medbourne, Colonel Killigrew, and Mr. Gascoigne, were early lovers of the Widow Wycherly. In fact, they had once been on the point of cutting each other's throats for her sake.

"My dear old friends," said Dr. Heidegger, motioning them to be seated. "I want you to help me with one of those little experiments with which I amuse myself here in my study."

If all stories were true, Dr. Heidegger's study must have been a very curious place. It was a dim, old-fashioned room, full of cobwebs and sprinkled with dust. Around the walls stood several bookcases. In the farthest corner was a closet with its door ajar, within which appeared a skeleton. Between two of the bookcases hung a huge mirror in a dirty old frame, the subject of many wonderful stories. It was said that the spirits of all the doctor's dead patients lived within this frame, and would stare him in the face whenever he looked into it. The opposite side of the room was decorated with a painting of a young lady, dressed in the faded loveliness of silk and satin. Fifty years before, Dr. Heidegger had been on the point of marriage with this young lady. But, being taken with some slight illness, she had swallowed one of her lover's prescriptions, and died on the bridal evening. The greatest curiosity of the study remains to be mentioned: a huge black book, held together with large silver clasps. There were no letters on the back, and nobody could tell the title of the book. But it was well known to be a book of magic. And once, when a maid had lifted it to brush away the dust, the skeleton had rattled in its closet, the picture of the young lady had leaned forward from its frame, and several ghostly faces had peeped out from the mirror.

Such was Dr. Heidegger's study. On the summer afternoon of our tale, a small round table stood in the center of the room. On it was a cut-glass vase of beautiful form. The sunshine came through the window, between the heavy faded curtains, and fell directly across this vase. A mild glow was reflected from the vase on the gray faces of the five old people who sat around. Four small glasses were also on the table.

"My dear old friends," repeated Dr. Heidegger, "may I count on your aid in making a very curious experiment?"

Now Dr. Heidegger was a very strange old gentleman. When the doctor's four guests heard him talk of his experiment, they thought of nothing especially wonderful. Perhaps the murder of a mouse in an air pump or some similar nonsense, with which he was always bothering his friends. But without waiting for a reply, Dr. Heidegger walked across the room to the black book which all supposed to be a book of magic. Undoing the silver clasps, he opened it and took from its pages a rose, or what was once a rose. Now the green leaves and red petals had become brown. The ancient flower seemed ready to crumble to dust in the doctor's hands.

"This rose," said Dr. Heidegger, with a sigh, "this same dry and crumbling flower, blossomed five and fifty years ago. It was given to me by Sylvia Ward, whose picture hangs there on the wall. I once meant to wear it at our wedding. Five and fifty years it has been treasured between the pages of this old book. Now, would you think it possible that this rose could ever bloom again?"

"Nonsense!" said the Widow Wycherly, with a toss of her head. "You might as well ask whether an old woman's wrinkled face could ever bloom again."

"See!" answered Dr. Heidegger.

He uncovered the vase, and threw the faded rose into the water which it held. At first, it lay lightly on the surface. Soon, however, a strange change began. The crushed and dried petals stirred, and took on a deepening red color, as if the flower were waking from a deathlike sleep. The slender stalk and leaves became green. There was the rose of fifty years, looking as fresh as when Sylvia Ward had first given it to her lover!

"That is certainly a very pretty trick," said the doctor's friends. "Tell us, how was it done?"

"Did you never hear of the Fountain of Youth," asked Dr. Heidegger, "which Ponce de León, the Spanish explorer, went in search of two or three centuries ago?"

"But did Ponce de León ever find it?" said the Widow Wycherly.

" No," answered Dr. Heidegger, "for he never looked in the right place. The famous Fountain of Youth, if I have been told correctly, is in the southern part of Florida, not far from Lake Macaco. It is covered over by several giant magnolias, hundreds of years old, but still as fresh as violets. A friend of mine, knowing my curiosity in such matters, has sent me the water you see in the vase."

"Ahem!" said Colonel Killigrew, who believed not a word of the doctor's story. "And what is the effect of this fluid on a human being?"

"You shall judge for yourself, my dear colonel," replied Dr. Heidegger. "All of you, my friends, are welcome to as much of this fluid as may give you back the bloom of youth. For my own part, having had much trouble in growing old, I am in no hurry to grow young again. With your permission, therefore, I will only watch the experiment."

While he spoke, Dr. Heidegger had been filling the four small glasses with the water of the Fountain of Youth. Little bubbles were continually rising from the bottoms of the glasses, and bursting in silvery spray at the surface.

"Before you drink, my old friends," said Dr. Heidegger, "I have a good idea. With the experience of a lifetime to direct you, you might draw up a few general rules for your guidance, in passing a second time through the dangers of youth. Think what a sin and shame it would be to waste a second chance! Having lived one life, you should become models of goodness and wisdom to all the young people of the age!"

The doctor's four old friends made no answer, so very ridiculous was the idea that they should ever go wrong again. With shaking hands, they raised the glasses to their lips. The fluid could not have been given to four human beings who needed it more. They looked as if they had never known what youth or pleasure was. They looked as if they had always been the gray, miserable people who now sat around the doctor's table. They drank the water, and placed their glasses back on the table.

There was an almost immediate improvement in the old people, as if a sudden glow of cheerful sunshine had brightened all their faces at once. There was a healthful glow on their cheeks, instead of the gray color that had made them look so corpse-like. The Widow Wycherly adjusted her cap, for she felt almost like a woman again.

"Give us more of this wonderful water!" cried they, eagerly. "We are younger—but we are still too old! Quick—give us more!"

"Patience, patience!" said Dr. Heidegger, who sat watching the experiment with coolness. "You have been a long time growing old. Surely, you might be content to grow young in half an hour! But the water is at your service."

Again he filled their glasses with the fluid, enough of which still remained to turn half the old people in the city young again. While the bubbles were still sparkling on the surface, the doctor's four guests snatched their glasses from the table. They swallowed the water at a single gulp. Even while the drink was passing down their throats, their eyes grew clear and bright. A dark shade deepened on their silver heads. They sat around the table, three gentlemen and a woman of middle age.

"My dear widow, you are charming!" cried Colonel Killigrew. His eyes had been fixed upon her face as the shadows of age left it, like darkness from the rosy daybreak.

The widow knew, of old, that Colonel Killigrew's compliments were not always the truth. She stood up and ran to the mirror, still dreading that the ugly face of an old woman would meet her eyes. Meanwhile, the three gentlemen behaved as they had many years before. The water of the Fountain of Youth had removed the weight of years. Mr. Gascoigne's mind seemed to run on political topics. He spoke long sentences about patriotism, national glory, and the people's rights. Colonel Killigrew sang a drinking song, while his eyes wandered toward the figure of the Widow Wycherly. On the other side of the table, Mr. Medbourne was figuring in dollars and cents the cost of supplying the East Indies with ice. He spoke of harnessing a team of whales to the polar icebergs.

As for the Widow Wycherly, she stood before the mirror smiling at her own reflection. She greeted it as the friend whom she loved better than all the world. She put her face close to the glass, to see whether some long-remembered wrinkle had really disappeared. She examined whether the snow had entirely melted from her hair. At last, turning away, she came with a sort of dancing step to the table.

"My dear old doctor," cried she, "pray give me another glass!"

"Certainly my dear madam, certainly!" replied the doctor. "See! I have already filled the glasses."

There, in fact, stood the four glasses, full of this wonderful water. The four guests took their third drink of the Fountain of Youth. The next moment, the happy blood of young life shot through their veins. They were now in the prime of youth. Age, with its miserable cares and sorrows and diseases, was remembered only as the trouble of a dream. Now they had joyfully awakened. They felt like new-created people in a new-created world.

Youth had now captured them all. They were a group of happy youngsters. The strongest effect of their happiness was an urge to joke about the sickness and sadness that had so lately been theirs. They laughed loudly at their old-fashioned clothes. One limped across the floor like an old, old grandfather. Then all shouted joyfully and leaped about the room. The Widow Wycherly—if so fresh a girl could be called a widow—ran up to the doctor's chair, with a look of mischief in her rosy face.

"Doctor, you dear old soul," cried she, "get up and

dance with me!" And then the four young people laughed louder than ever.

"Pray excuse me," answered the doctor quietly. "I am old, and my dancing days were over long ago. But any of these young gentlemen will be glad for so pretty a partner."

"Dance with me, Clara!" cried Colonel Killigrew.

"No, no, I will be her partner!" shouted Mr. Gascoigne.

"She promised me her hand, fifty years ago!" exclaimed Mr. Medbourne.

They all gathered around her. One caught both her hands in his—another threw his arm about her waist—the third buried his head among her shining curls. She blushed, panted, struggled, and laughed, her warm breath on each of their faces in turn. She tried to free herself, yet still remained in their hold. Excited to madness by the giggles of the girl-widow, the three men began to exchange threatening looks. Still keeping hold of their fair prize, they reached fiercely for one another's throats. As they struggled back and forth, the table was overturned, and the vase dashed into a thousand pieces. The precious Water of Youth flowed in a bright stream across the floor, touching the wings of a dying butterfly. The insect fluttered lightly through the room and settled on the snowy head of Dr. Heidegger.

"Come, come, gentlemen!—come, Madam Wycherly," exclaimed the doctor, "I really must ask you to behave."

They stood still and shivered; for it seemed as if Father Time were calling them back from their sunny youth. They looked at old Dr. Heidegger, who sat holding the rose he had rescued from among the pieces of the broken vase. At the motion of his hand, the four rioters took their seats. Their exercise had tired them, youthful though they were.

"My poor Sylvia's rose!" exclaimed Dr. Heidegger, holding it up. "It appears to be fading again."

And so it was. Even while the guests were looking at it,

the flower continued to dry up. Soon it became as old and brown as when the doctor had first thrown it into the vase. He shook off the few drops which clung to its petals.

"I love it as well this way as in its youthful freshness," he said, pressing the withered rose to his withered lips. While he spoke, the butterfly fluttered down from the doctor's snowy head, and fell upon the floor.

His guests shivered again. A strange cold feeling was creeping slowly over them all. They looked at one another, and saw that each moment left a deepening wrinkle where none had been before. Had it been a trick? Had the changes of a lifetime been crowded into so brief a space? Were they now four old people again, sitting with their old friend, Dr. Heidegger?

"Are we grown old again, so soon?" cried they, sorrowfully.

In truth they had. The Water of Youth had had but a brief effect. Yes! they were old again. The widow put her skinny hands before her face, and wished that the coffin lid were over it, since it could be no longer beautiful.

"Yes, friends, you are old again," said Dr. Heidegger, "and the Water of Youth is all spilled on the ground. Well—I regret it not. For if the fountain were at my very doorstep, I would not lean over to touch my lips to it. No I wouldn't, even if its effect were for years instead of moments. This is the lesson you have taught me!"

But the doctor's four friends had taught no such lesson to themselves. They decided right away to make a journey to Florida, and drink morning, noon, and night, from the Fountain of Youth.

Recall

1. Dr. Heidegger's study is described as being (a) ordinary (b) neat (c) curious.
2. The three old men invited to Dr. Heidegger's study are alike in that they all once (a) were in love with the Widow Wycherly (b) loved Sylvia Ward (c) had been in politics.
3. All four persons who come to Dr. Heidegger's study are (a) unfortunate but happy (b) unfortunate and melancholy (c) fortunate but melancholy.
4. In Dr. Heidegger's study hangs a portrait of his (a) sister (b) mother (c) bride-to-be.
5. First to be treated with the magic water is a (a) man (b) woman (c) rose.
6. According to Dr. Heidegger, the Fountain of Youth is in (a) Texas (b) Florida (c) California.
7. Before his guests drink the water, Dr. Heidegger suggests that they (a) change into more youthful clothes (b) have their pictures taken (c) draw up some rules based on experience.
8. After the first drink, Dr. Heidegger's guests are (a) eager for more (b) satisfied (c) sorry.
9. After the second drink, Dr. Heidegger's guests start (a) talking about their younger selves (b) crying about their younger selves (c) acting like their younger selves.
10. After the third drink, Dr. Heidegger's guests start (a) blaming Dr. Heidegger for their troubles (c) laughing and looking for fun (d) remembering rules of good behavior.

11. A fight starts over (a) the rest of the water (b) the Widow Wycherly (c) the rose.

12. After the riot, Dr. Heidegger's guests (a) become old again (b) stay young (c) keep growing younger and become babies.

13. The one person who learns a lesson from the experiment is (a) Dr. Heidegger (b) the Widow Wycherly (c) Mr. Gascoigne.

14. At the end of the story, the four old people (a) wish never again to drink the magic water (b) agree that they've made fools of themselves (c) plan a trip to Florida.

Infer

15. Dr. Heidegger conducted his experiment (a) to see if the butterfly would live (b) to see what his guests would do (c) to discover the formula for the magic water.

16. Dr. Heidegger chose only miserable people for his experiment because (a) they would have made more mistakes in life to correct (b) he knew no happy people (c) unhappy people are more easily fooled.

17. The "lesson" Dr. Heidegger speaks of at the end of the story is that (a) experience is the best teacher (b) old people really do not want to become young again (c) if given a second chance in life, people will repeat the mistakes of their youth.

18. Throughout the story, Dr. Heidegger's general attitude is one of (a) great hope (b) coolness and sadness (c) feverish excitement.

19. The author suggests that if the effect of the magic water had lasted forever, the new lives of Dr. Heidegger's guests would have been (a) different from the old lives (b) happy (c) unhappy.

20. The author's main purpose in writing the story was probably to (a) persuade us that the Fountain of Youth still exists (b) get us to consider the lesson learned by Dr. Heidegger (c) tell us a story he believed to be true.

Vocabulary Review

Below are *italicized* words from the story followed by sentences with blanks. On your paper, write the numeral of each sentence and the words that best fill the blanks. Use each word only once.

clasps	*magnolia*	*polar*	*withered*
crumble	*melancholy*	*prime*	

1. In full bloom, the flowers on a ——— tree are at their ———.
2. A month later, the flowers will have ——— and will be ready to ——— into dust.
3. The huge globe was supported by two metal ——— near its ——— regions.
4. ——— thoughts filled the old man's mind.

Critical Thinking

1. The author takes some time early in the story to describe Dr. Heidegger's study as a magic place. Why do you think he does this? What does it add to the story?

2. After the second drink, the three men all start talking foolishly about their past interests. What does the Widow Wycherly do at this point? (Look back if you have to.) In your opinion, is she being foolish too? Why? What is the author suggesting about the interests and concerns of many women? Do you agree? Explain.

3. Do you agree with the "lesson" Dr. Heidegger says he's learned? Explain.

4. Think about the very old people that you know. How many could really be described as "melancholy" and "miserable"? How many do you think would really accept a chance to live their lives over again? Why do you think this is so?

5. Suppose you could go back a few years and live your life over again. Think of two or three changes you'd like to make. Do you think that you could make these changes *knowing no more than you knew at the time?* Do you think that *even with the experience you now have* you could make these changes? Explain fully.

The Holiday Man

Richard Matheson

JULY 4TH DEATHS ESTIMATED AT 510

375 ACCIDENTAL DEATHS PREDICTED FOR MEMORIAL DAY WEEKEND

Everyone has seen headlines like these. Just before important holidays like "the Fourth," the sad predictions are in the newspapers and on the radio. And if you've noticed, the figures are usually pretty close to being right. But did you ever ask yourself "How can they tell?" *That question is answered in the next story. Fasten your seatbelts before you read this one.*

Vocabulary Preview

CUBICLE (KYOO-buh-kul) a small office that is part of a larger room
• Each of the guidance teachers worked in a small *cubicle.*

ELECTROCUTED (il-LEK truh-kyoo-tud) killed by electricity
• Three people were *electrocuted* when the power line fell on them during the storm.

EN ROUTE (en-ROOT) on the way
• The Millers passed through Detroit *en route* to Chicago.

SUITE (SWEET) a group of connected rooms, often in a hotel
• The President stayed in a *suite* on the top floor of the Mark Hopkins hotel.

SUPERIOR (soo-PEER-ee-ur) a person of high rank or authority
• Mom asked her *superior* at work for the day off.

VAPOR (VAY-pur) mist or steam
• The air in the busy kitchen was filled with *vapor* from boiling water.

WRITHED (RITHED) twisted and turned in pain
• The injured man *writhed* on the street while the car which struck him sped away.

"YOU'LL BE LATE," SHE SAID.

He leaned back tiredly in his chair.

"I know," he answered.

They were in the kitchen having breakfast. David hadn't eaten much. Mostly, he'd drunk black coffee and stared at the tablecloth. There were thin lines running through it that looked like highways.

"Well?" she said.

He shivered and took his eyes from the tablecloth.

"Yes," he said. "All right."

He kept sitting there.

"David," she said.

"I know, I know," he said. "I'll be late." He wasn't angry. There was no anger left in him.

"You certainly will," she said, buttering her toast: She spread thick raspberry jam, then bit off a piece and chewed it cracklingly.

David got up and walked across the kitchen. At the door he stopped and turned. He stared at the back of her head.

"Why couldn't I?" he asked again.

"Because you can't," she said. "That's all."

"But *why*?"

"Because they need you," she said. "Because they pay you well and you couldn't do anything else. Isn't it obvious?"

"They could find someone else."

"Oh, stop it," she said. "You know they couldn't."

He closed his hands into fists. "Why should I be the one?" he asked.

She didn't answer. She sat eating her toast.

"Jean?"

"There's nothing more to say," she said, chewing. She turned around. "Now, will you go?" she said. "You shouldn't be late today." David felt a chill in his flesh.

"No," he said, "not today."

He walked out of the kitchen and went upstairs. There, he brushed his teeth, polished his shoes, and put on a tie. Before eight he was down again. He went into the kitchen.

"Good-bye," he said.

She tilted up her cheek for him, and he kissed it. " 'Bye dear," she said. "Have a—" She stopped.

"—nice day?" he finished for her. "Thank you." He turned away. "I'll have a lovely day."

Long ago he had stopped driving a car. Mornings he walked to the railroad station. He didn't even like to ride with someone else or take a bus.

At the station he stood outside on the platform waiting for the train. He had no newspaper. He never bought them anymore.

"Mornin', Garrett."

He turned and saw Henry Coulter who also worked in the city. Coulter patted him on the back.

"Good morning," David said.

"How's it goin'?" Coulter asked.

"Fine. Thank you."

"Good. Lookin' forward to the Fourth?"

David swallowed. "Well . . ." he began.

"Myself, I'm takin' the family to the woods," said Coulter. "No lousy fireworks for us. Pilin' into the old bus and headin' out till the fireworks are over."

"Driving," said David.

"Yes, *sir*," said Coulter. "Far as we can."

It began by itself. No, he thought; *not now.* He forced it back into its darkness.

"—tising business," Coulter finished.

"What?" he asked.

"Said I trust things are goin' well in the advertising business."

David cleared his throat.

"Oh, yes," he said. "Fine." He always forgot about the lie he'd told Coulter.

When the train arrived, he sat in the No Smoking car knowing that Coulter always smoked a cigar en route. He didn't want to sit with Coulter. Not now.

All the way to the city he sat looking out the window. Mostly he watched road and highway traffic; but once, while the train rattled over a bridge, he stared down at the surface of a lake. Once he put his head back and looked up at the sun.

He was actually to the elevator when he stopped.

"Up?" said the man in the maroon uniform. He looked at David steadily. "Up?" he said. Then he closed the rolling doors.

David stood motionless. People began to cluster around him. In a moment, he turned and shouldered by them, pushing through the revolving door. As he came out, the oven heat of July surrounded him. He moved along the sidewalk like a man asleep. On the next block he entered a bar.

Inside, it was cold and dim. There were no customers. Not even the bartender was in view. David sank down in the shadow of a booth and took his hat off. He leaned his head back and closed his eyes.

He couldn't do it. He simply could not go up to his office. No matter what Jean said, no matter what anyone said. He clasped his hands on the table edge and squeezed them until the fingers were pressed dry of blood. He just *wouldn't.*

"Help you?" asked a voice.

David opened his eyes. The bartender was standing by the booth looking down at him.

"Yes, uh . . . beer," he said. He hated beer, but he knew he had to buy something for the privilege of sitting in the chilly silence undisturbed. He wouldn't drink it.

The bartender brought the beer, and David paid for it. Then when the bartender had gone, he began to turn the glass slowly on the tabletop. While he was doing this it began again. With a gasp, he pushed it away. *No!* he told it.

In a while he got up and left the bar. It was past ten. That didn't matter, of course. They knew he was always late. They knew he always tried to break away from it and never could.

His office was at the back of the suite, a small soundproof cubicle furnished only with a rug, a couch, and a small desk on which lay pencils and white paper. It was all he needed. Once he'd had a secretary, but he hadn't liked the idea of her sitting outside the door and listening to him scream.

No one saw him enter. He let himself in from the hall through a private door. Inside, he relocked the door, then took off his suit coat, and laid it across the desk. It was stuffy in the office so he walked across the floor and pulled up the window.

Far below, the city moved. He stood watching it. How many of them? he thought.

Sighing heavily, he turned. Well, he was here. There was no point in hesitating any longer. He was committed now. The best thing was to get it over and clear out.

He drew the blinds, walked over to the couch, and lay down. He fussed a little with the pillow, then stretched once and was still. Almost immediately, he felt his limbs going numb.

It began.

He did not stop it now. It trickled on his brain liked melted ice. It rushed like winter wind. It spun like blizzard vapor. It leaped and ran and exploded, and his mind was filled with it. He grew rigid and began to gasp, his chest twitching with breath. His hands drew in like white claws, clutching and scratching at the couch. He shivered and groaned and writhed. Finally, he screamed. He screamed for a very long while.

When it was done, he lay limp and motionless on the couch, his eyes like balls of frozen glass. When he could, he raised his arm and looked at his wrist watch. It was almost two.

He struggled to his feet. His bones felt like lead, but he managed to stumble to his desk.

There he wrote on a sheet of paper and, when he was finished, slumped across the desk and fell into exhausted sleep.

Later, he woke up and took the sheet of paper to his superior who, looking it over, nodded.

"Four hundred eighty-six, huh?" the superior said. "You're sure of that?"

"I'm sure," said David quietly. "I watched every one." He didn't mention that Coulter and his family were among them.

"All right," said his superior, "let's see now. Four hundred fifty-two from traffic accidents, eighteen from drowning, seven from sunstroke, three from fireworks, six from other causes."

Such as a little girl being burned to death, David thought. Such as a baby boy eating ant poison. Such as a woman being electrocuted; a man dying of snake bite.

"Well," his superior said, "let's make it—oh, four hundred and fifty. It's always impressive when more people die than we predict."

"Of course," David said.

The item was on the front page of all the newspapers that afternoon. While David was riding home, the man in front of him turned to his neighbor and said, "What I'd like to know is—*how can they tell?*"

David got up and went back on the platform at the end of the car. Until he got off, he stood there listening to the train wheels and thinking about Labor Day.

Recall

1. The story takes place just before (a) Memorial Day (b) the Fourth of July (c) Labor Day.
2. David goes to work by (a) car (b) train (c) bus.
3. David is late to work because he (a) has an accident (b) enjoys drinking beer (c) is terrified of his job.
4. David's job involves (a) testing dangerous drugs (b) "seeing" and predicting accidents (c) studying the effects of advertising.
5. "The item . . . on the front page of all the newspapers" is (a) the effect of a new drug (b) the accident prediction (c) a report on advertising.

Infer

6. The attitude of David's wife can best be described as (a) businesslike (b) sympathetic (c) fearful.
7. At the end of the first section of the story, David tells his wife, "I'll have a lovely day." When he speaks these words, he (a) means what he says (b) means just the opposite (c) is unsure of what he means.

8. The reason David no longer drives a car is probably that (a) he enjoys talking to people like Henry Coulter on the train (b) his wife insists on driving (c) he is terrified of accidents.
9. David has told Coulter that he was in the advertising business because (a) he wanted to make Coulter jealous (b) he wanted his real occupation to remain secret (c) it was true at the time.
10. At the end of the story, we know that (a) Coulter and his family will be in a bad accident (b) David is looking forward to Labor Day (c) David's wife will soon die.

Vocabulary Review

Write on your paper the word in italics that belongs in each sentence below. Use each word only once.

cubicle	*en route*	*superior*	*writhe*
electrocuted	*suite*	*vapor*	

1. The Republican Party rented a hotel ——— as its headquarters.
2. The clerk said he would have to ask his ——— if the suit could be delivered.
3. The store manager worked in a small ——— in a back room of the store.
4. There was so much——— in the air that we couldn't see across the river.
5. Did you see anything interesting ——— to San Francisco?
6. Hit by a wild pitch, the batter began to ——— in pain.
7. Murderers used to be hanged, gassed, or ———.

Critical Thinking

1. Why does David continue with a job he desperately wants to quit? Does anything in the story suggest that perhaps he can't quit, no matter how much he wants to? If so, what?

2. When did you first understand exactly what David's job was? The story is full of small clues. Look back and find the clue in the fourth paragraph. How many others can you find in the story?

3. Other people besides David use "supernatural" methods to try to predict future events. What are some of these methods? What are some names for these people? Do you believe that anyone can really predict future events? Explain.

Starbride

Anthony Boucher

Not too long ago, on July 20, 1969, a human being landed on the moon for the first time. What do you think the next big space adventure will be? What would happen if the United States sent an army to take over a planet like Mars? At first, certainly, there'd be a lot of talk about our conquest of the Martian people. America's empire would extend far out into space. The government might create a "Federal Council" to make important decisions about the new colony. A "Colonial Administration"—or "C.A." for short—might govern the Martians. Let's join the future now through the frisky imagination of Anthony Boucher.

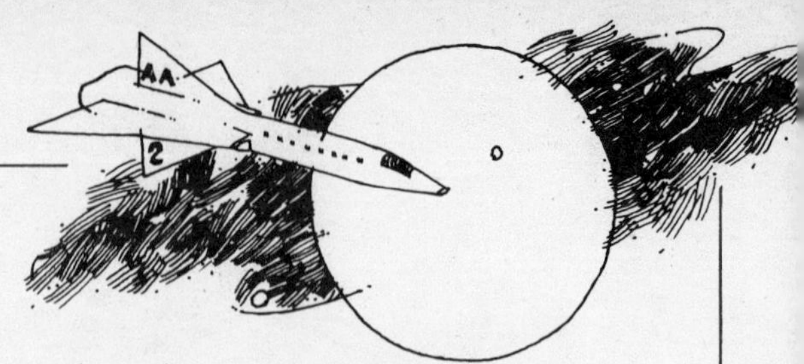

Vocabulary Preview

BOUND (BOWND) fixed to a certain place; prevented from leaving

• Mom told me I was house-*bound* until my cold got better.

CIVILIZATION (siv-uh-luh-ZAY-shun) the total way of life of a nation or larger group

• Scientists have dug up ruins in Peru that give many clues to the *civilization* of the Incas.

CONQUERED (KON-kurd) defeated in war and taken over

• France was a *conquered* country during most of World War II.

DECEASED (dee-SEEST) dead

• The Post Office stamps "DECEASED" on envelopes addressed to dead people.

NATIVE (NAY-tiv) belonging to a place by birth or origin

• Sergeant Miller went to Japan and married a *native* girl.

PSYCHIATRIST (suh-KI-uh-trist) a doctor who specializes in treating the minds of patients

• Butch seems happier now that he's seeing a *psychiatrist*.

TROOPS (TROOPS) soldiers

• The British *troops* wore red coats.

I ALWAYS KNEW, EVER SINCE WE WERE IN school together, that he'd love me some day; and I knew somehow too that I'd always be in second place. I didn't really care either, but I never guessed then what I'd come second to: a native girl from a conquered planet.

I couldn't guess because those school days were before the Conquest and the Empire, back in the days when we used to talk about a rocket to a moon and never dreamed how fast it would all happen after that rocket.

When it did all begin to happen I thought at first what I was going to come second to was Space itself. But that wasn't for long and now Space can never take him away from me and neither can she, not really, because she's dead.

But he sits there by the waters and talks and I can't even hate her, because she was a woman too, and she loved him too, and that was what she died of.

He doesn't talk about it as often as he used to, and I suppose that's something. It's only when the fever's bad, or he's tried to talk to the Federal Council again about our colonies on other planets. That's worse than the fever.

He sits there and he looks up at her star and he says, "But damn it, they're *people.* Oh, I was like all the rest at first; I was expecting some kind of monster even after the reports from the Conquest troops. And when I saw that they looked almost like us, and after all those months in the space ship, with the old regulation against mixed crews . . ."

He has to tell it. The psychiatrist explained that to me very carefully. I'm only glad it doesn't come so often now.

"Everybody in Colonial Administration was doing it," he says. "They'd pick the girl that came the closest to somebody back home and they'd go through the Vlnian marriage ceremony—which of course isn't recognized legally under the C.A., at least not where we're concerned."

I've never asked him whether she came close to me.

"It's a beautiful ceremony, though," he says. "That's what I keep telling the Council: Vln had a much higher level of pre-Conquest civilization than we'll admit. She taught me poetry and music that . . ."

I know it all by heart now. All the poetry and all the music. It's strange and sad and like nothing you ever dreamed of . . . and like everything you ever dreamed.

"It was living with her that made me know," he says. "Being with her, part of her, knowing that there was nothing bad, nothing ugly about green flesh and white next to each other."

No, that's what he used to say. He doesn't say that part any more. He does love me. "They've got to understand!" he says, looking at her star.

The psychiatrist explained why he's feeling guilty; but I still don't see why he has to have guilt. He couldn't help it. He wanted to come back. He meant to come back. Only that was the trip he got space fever, and of course after that he was planet-bound for life.

"She had a funny name," he says. "I never could pronounce it right—all vowels. So I called her Starbride, even though she said that was foolish—we both belonged to the same star, the sun, even if we were of different planets. I tell you the average level of Vlnian civilization . . ."

And I still think of it as her star when he sits there and looks at it. I can't keep things like that straight, and he does call her Starbride.

"I swore to come back before the child was born," he said. "I swore by her God and by mine and He heard me under both names. And she said very simply, 'If you don't, I'll die.' That's all, just 'I'll die.' And then we drank native wine and sang folksongs all night and went to bed in the dawn."

And he doesn't need to tell me about his letter to her, but he does. He doesn't need to because I sent it myself. It was the first thing he thought of when he came out of the fever and saw the calendar and I wrote it down for him and sent it. And it came back with the C.A. stamp: *Deceased* and that was all.

"And I don't know how she died," he says, "or even whether the child was born. Try to find out anything about a native from a Colonial Administrator! They've got to be made to realize . . ."

Then he usually doesn't talk for a while. He just sits there by the waters and looks up at the blue star and sings their sad folksongs with the funny names: *Saint Louis Blues* and *Barbara Allen* and *Lover, Come Back To Me.*

And after a while I say, "I'm not planet-bound. Some day when you're well enough for me to leave you I'll go to Vln—"

"*'Earth',*" he says, almost as though it was a love-word and not just a funny noise. "That's their name for Vln. She called herself an Earth woman, and she called me her Martian."

"I'll go to Earth," I say, only I never can pronounce it quite right and he always laughs a little, "and I'll find your child and I'll bring it back to you."

Then he turns and smiles at me and after a while we leave the waters of the canal and go inside again away from her blue star. Those are the times when I can almost endure the pain of being second in his heart, second to a white Starbride far away and dead on a planet called Earth.

Recall

1. The narrator (the person who tells the story) is (a) seeing a psychiatrist (b) concerned about her husband (c) planning revenge on Starbride.
2. The narrator's husband has (a) returned from another planet the day before (b) brought Starbride home (c) married a girl on another planet.
3. The husband cannot go back to the other planet because (a) he has space fever and is planet-bound (b) the people there would kill him (c) the narrator won't let him.
4. If the husband were to go back, he would probably (a) bring Starbride home (b) try to discover if his child were alive (c) bring Starbride and his child home.
5. According to the psychiatrist, it does the husband good to (a) sing the songs Starbride taught him (b) see Starbride occasionally (c) talk about his troubles.

Infer

6. The story is supposed to happen (a) in our lifetimes (b) about a hundred years from now (c) in the far, far distant future.
7. The narrator's attitude toward her husband is best described as (a) dishonest (b) bitter (c) understanding.
8. The big surprise at the end of the story is that (a) Starbride's planet, Vln, is really Earth (b) the narrator offers to get the child (c) the husband smiles.
9. The narrator is (a) white (b) black (c) green.
10. One of the story's main points concerns (a) pride (b) the value of folk music (c) brotherhood.

Vocabulary Review

1. Mr. Tomomi Moto, who lives in Los Angeles, California, is not a *native* Japanese. Mr. Moto probably (a) is a citizen of Japan (b) was born in Japan (c) was not born in Japan.
2. A *deceased psychiatrist* could be called a (a) diseased mind (b) dead doctor (c) decimal system.
3. "RED SOX *CONQUER* TIGERS, 5-3." This headline would probably please (a) a Red Sox fan (b) a Tiger fan (c) anyone who favors war.
4. Parents with young children often feel house-*bound*. In other words, they feel (a) like cleaning house (b) like buying a house (c) tied to the house.
5. Government troops nearly destroyed the *civilization* of the Sioux Indians. In other words, (a) taxes took away the Indians' wealth (b) soldiers almost ruined the Indians' way of life (c) teachers nearly changed the Indians' language.

Critical Thinking

1. Describe the feelings of the narrator toward her husband and toward Starbride. Do you admire her attitudes? Why, or why not?
2. What does the husband seem to admire most about the civilization on Earth? Do you think he's right, or would you place more value on some other part of our civilization? Explain.
3. Why does the husband feel guilty? Does his guilt make sense to you? Explain.

4. Explain how the sudden surprise, or "twist," at the end of the story might make us think differently about the future of space travel. What common beliefs does the author of the story refuse to take for granted?

5. "Starbride" was written before we sent a rocket to the moon. That part of the story has already come true. Do you think space travel among the planets will ever come true? Explain your answer.

The Canvas Bag

Alan E. Nourse

Ready to shift gears? Let's go from forward to reverse, from the future to the past. Did you ever try to remember something that happened long, long ago? You dig into your memory, but the details that you want stay buried. After a while you turn up one detail . . . and another . . . and still another. Then suddenly, and without much effort on your part, everything comes rushing back. Why, you remember every little detail! You're amazed to find yourself living in a past you didn't know you knew. This is exactly what happens to Joe Baker in the following story. Well, not exactly *what happens—get ready for a surprise.*

Vocabulary Preview

BARRIER (BAIR-ee-ur) something that blocks the way or keeps people from passing
• The police set up *barriers* around the bombed bank.

BOARDINGHOUSE (BOR-ding HOUSE) a rooming house; a place that has inexpensive rooms for rent
• Uncle Al lived in a *boardinghouse* before he was married.

CANVAS (KAN-vus) a kind of very heavy cloth
• The old tent was made of *canvas.*

DEPRESSION (dip-PRESH-un) a period when many people are out of work
• Ask an older person about the bad *depression* of the 1930's.

DRIFTED (DRIF-tid) moved here and there without any particular goal or purpose
• After high school, my brother *drifted* around the country for two years.

DRIFTER (DRIF-tur) a person who drifts
• Then Bill decided to stop being a *drifter* and settle down.

TINKLING (TINK-ling) making a light, clear sound
• The ice cubes *tinkling* in the glass of water sounded musical.

THE TELEPHONE RANG JUST AS JOE BAKER got himself settled in the bathtub. He growled something nasty and dashed the length of the rooming house hallway to his little room at the end, bathrobe flying, splattering water far and wide as he reached for the telephone. Then Jeannie's voice was tinkling in his ear; his anger disappeared, and his heart skipped twice.

Jeannie was laughing. "I must have dragged you out of the shower! You sound like you've been jumping over barriers."

"Many barriers," said Joe, slapping at the water running down his leg. His feet were planted in a spreading puddle. "There's nothing wrong—is there?"

"Nothing too bad." Jeannie's voice was warm. "I'll have to be late tonight, is all. Maybe an hour or more—I don't know. Frankie's decided that *this* is the night we'll have to really clean up the diner. No other night will do. And you know Frankie."

Joe shook the water out of his ears, and cursed Frankie silently. A chill of disappointment stabbed through him. There would be an hour's delay in their dinner date. But then, he was sure he heard the same disappointment in Jeannie's voice, and he felt somewhat better. It was almost as if she knew what a special date it was going to be. "How about nine, then? I'll meet you there."

"We should be finished by then. I'll be hungry, too."

"Sky's the limit tonight. Even on barriers to jump." He wondered how a girl who spent all day dishing out food could bear to look at it at night, much less eat it.

Jeannie's laugh was still in his ears as he hung up. He

looked sadly around the room. An *extra* hour to kill. He could hardly bear it. It was an ugly room with a single window that stared out on the main street, catching the hot Indiana sun. Not a bad room, if you liked cheap boarding-houses. From the window he could see the whole town before him. He stared down for a moment before turning away, allowing his mind to go back to his first view of the small town, the day he'd dropped off the freight car six weeks before.

A grubby little dump town, he had thought. A good place to stop for the night, and move on. They probably wouldn't like drifters around here, anyway. Nothing unusual, his thinking that—the usual thoughts that went through his mind when he hit a little Midwest town with its dusty streets and its dirty wooden houses. It was even an ordinary-looking diner where he had been sitting, when the girl behind the counter had come over, and he had looked up and seen Jeannie.

He gave a little laugh now, and took clean clothes from the dresser. A new shirt had always been a problem for Joe; he struggled into it bravely, grinning at himself in the mirror. So very much could happen in six short weeks! Your ideas of towns and people and everything could change so rapidly. He whistled a little tune, studying his wide tanned face and wild brown hair as he tied the tie. Not a bad face, Joe Baker. Not bad at all. You could see how a girl might go for it. And tonight, she simply *had* to go for it. He'd never asked a girl to marry him before in his whole life. She couldn't refuse, not tonight.

But the thought of marriage made him feel a bit strange. It was bound to happen sometime, he had told himself. A man can't tramp the roads forever. Someday the time would come to stop. It had always been sometime in the dim, distant future, with Joe. But it wasn't any more. Tonight the time had come.

And then his eye fell on the little blue canvas bag on the floor in the corner.

He blinked at the bag. The bag blinked back at him. He gave a nervous laugh, and kicked the bag. It went sliding across the floor.

"Good-by, Bag," he said happily. "I won't need *you* any more. Our days on the road are over."

For a girl who had worked all evening, Jeannie was bright and cheerful when Joe met her coming out of the diner. She was one of those amazing girls who never seem to run out of energy, and become the more beautiful the more work they do. She was slender and dark, with wide gray eyes set in a narrow face. Like a queen, Joe thought, as she came down the steps, or at least a princess. She kissed him lightly, and he slipped his arm around her as they walked around back to her old car.

"Let me take you away from all this," said Joe, politely. "Let me take you on the wings of the wind. The Pleasure Palace awaits."

She laughed, and Joe slipped easily into the driver's seat.

"The Spoon for dinner?" Jeannie asked.

"The Spoon? Not tonight. This is *our* night, and nothing but the best." He looked down at her and kissed her on the nose. "You know that place down by the bend of the river? Steaks an inch thick, they say, and dancing too." He slid the car out into the road traffic. "Tonight we celebrate."

"It's very, very expensive, I've heard."

"Eat, drink, and be merry."

Worry flashed in her gray eyes. "You're—you're not heading out again, are you, Joe?"

He smiled. "Not a chance. I'm thinking of giving up life on the road."

She snuggled closer and threw her head back happily. "For good?"

"For good."

"Then we *do* have something to celebrate."

The place was crowded when they arrived, but the waiter found them a table for two looking out on the river. Across the room a band was playing quietly as they ordered, and soon they were in each other's arms, dancing gracefully to the music. It was a strange world for Joe—a warm, soft world of love and sweet smells—and he could hardly keep his mind clear as the girl pressed her soft cheek to his. He had missed so much, all these years of drifting from town to town, never satisfied, never stopping. He had waited for years, and now he was sure, beyond doubt, that the long years of waiting had been worth it. "I've got a secret, Jeannie," he whispered as they moved into the shadows.

"Don't tell me," she whispered back.

"Why not?"

"Because then it wouldn't be a secret, would it?"

"But some secrets are for two people, they aren't any good for just one." Her ear was inches from his lips. "I love you, Jeannie. Did you know that?"

She nodded.

"I want you to marry me."

He thought he felt her arms tighten for a moment, and they danced silently, close together. But when she turned her face up to him, her eyes were serious and troubled. "Are you sure you want that?" she asked.

"I'm not fooling, Jeannie."

She turned her face away. "Oh, I know you're not, Joe,

but do you *know* what you want to do? Do you really want to stop drifting, take a house, settle down for good? Do you really think you could do that?"

"I wouldn't be asking you if I hadn't thought it over, would I?" There was a puzzled note in his voice, and he frowned. Something deep inside him had gone cold, a strange sort of pain he had never felt before. "I've been on the road for a long time, I know; but a man gets tired of it after a while. Sooner or later he finds a girl that makes it all seem silly." His words stopped; somehow, he couldn't get the right ones to come out. The coldness in his chest was deeper. "Look, Jeannie, the road is a hard life, there isn't any softness or friendship or happiness out there. Why would anybody choose it? Why should I ever want to go back?"

He broke off, realizing that he was raising his voice. He looked at Jeannie, and she looked away, shaking her head and leading the way back to their seats. She looked up at him strangely. "You don't have to convince me, Joe. *I* believe it." She paused. "I wonder if *you* believe it."

His voice choked in his throat. "I only know how I feel, and I know it's true. I wouldn't have asked you otherwise."

She nodded, staring at the tablecloth. Then she looked him straight in the eyes. "I want you to tell me something, Joe," she said quietly. "I want you to tell me how old you are."

Joe stared at her, and very slowly set down his glass. Something was drumming in his head, a frightening sound that chilled him to the bone. "Why, I'm . . . thirty-ish, or so," he said, wondering aloud. "Thirty-one, I think, or thirty-two." He blinked at her. "I don't know, it's somewhere around there."

"But can't you *remember,* Joe?" Her eyes were wide.

"Well, of course I can, I suppose! I had a birthday last

February." The drumming in his ears grew louder. "No, that was Pete Hower's birthday. We were on the road together. Funny guy, Pete. He——"

"*Please,* Joe!"

A chill ran up his back. It was as if he had suddenly looked over his shoulder and seen a huge pit opening up behind him. He saw Jeannie's worried face, and he tried hard, but his mind met with nothing except blank darkness. He stared at her in alarm. "Jeannie, *I can't remember!*"

"Oh, Joe! Think! You've got to!"

"But what difference does it make?"

"Joe——" The girl's voice was trembling, close to tears. "Think, Joe. Go back. Back to where you were before you came here, and where you went before that. Here—here's some paper. Write it down. Try to remember, Joe."

He took the pencil. Slowly, from the drumming in his head things were beginning to creep into his mind, strange things. "I—I just came East from North Dakota six weeks ago," he said. "Caught a freight train. Ran into some trouble with the cops and had a fight. And then I'd been in South Dakota for a while before that."

"How long?"

"Couple of months. I was working my way East, thought I'd work the docks for a while."

"And where were you before South Dakota?"

"California. Cab-driving job. I almost got killed; that made me want to head East. Came up from Mexico before that. And then before that there was the war."

A horrible thought flashed through Joe Baker's mind. A voice was screaming in his ear: *Which war, Joe, which war?*

Suddenly, in a flash of terror, he remembered. The muddy fog cleared from his mind, and his memory fell back and back and his face went white.

There was the fighting in Vietnam, and before that, in

Korea, and, going back, the bloody beaches of World War II——

And there was the girl in Pittsburgh who'd cleaned him out that night at Jardine's—God! that seemed like a hundred years ago! And the job in the woods up in Canada before that —

And the long depression years before that, with no money for a room —

And the job he'd lost when his boss had to go out of business—

And the run-in with the Boston cops in that liquor deal which couldn't go wrong —

And the cowboy job down through Wyoming and Colorado and Oklahoma before that—how long was that trip? Four years? Must have been, with all the time he'd wasted in Denver —

Joe Baker stared at the girl across the table from him, his mind screaming. He could almost see the blue canvas bag by his side, he could feel the excitement again as he had packed it full, ready for another move, and another, and another. . . . With a sudden rush he picked up the paper and pencil and began scratching down places, times, distances, with something digging into his chest as he wrote:

The end of World War I, and the long trip home from France —

The days of drifting through Europe right after 1900 —

The bitter feelings of the Kansas farmers when the railroads went through —

The pounding of horses' hoofs on the Nevada prairie, the wild screams of the Indians —

The crash of big guns, the bitter sharp voice of Civil War rifles at Gettysburg —

He remembered them. He remembered them all.

Joe Baker sat back in his chair, finally, his hands trembling. He couldn't believe it, of course. But it was true. He'd just never thought of it before. He'd drifted, from town to town, from job to job, anywhere the moment seemed to suggest. Drifted, and stopped for a while, and drifted again. He'd never thought of the past, for the past had always been filled with pain and loneliness. It had simply never occurred to him to stop and think how long he'd drifted, nor what might happen if he ever tried to stop.

And he had drifted for a hundred and fifty years.

He stared at the girl's frightened face. "You knew—somehow you knew."

She nodded. "I didn't know what it was. I knew you were *different,* somehow. At first I thought that you'd just been traveling a long time, that it was a part of a personality you'd built up on the road. I felt it the first moment I saw you. And then I began to realize that the difference was something else. But I didn't realize how long you've been going ——"

"But my face!" he cried. "My body! How could it be possible? Why aren't I old, dried up, dead?"

"I don't know."

"But it couldn't happen!"

Jeannie shook her head weakly. "There's something else far more important."

"What's that?"

"What makes you do it?"

"I tell you *I don't know.*"

"But you *must* have remembered the time passing!" she burst out.

Joe shook his head. "I just never stopped to think. Why should I have? There've never been friends, or family, or anyone to hang onto along the way. It never mattered what time it was, or what day it was. All that mattered was whether it was winter or summer, whether it was hot or cold, whether I was full or hungry. Jeannie, does it matter now? I love you, I want to stop, now, I want to marry you."

They were dancing again, and she was fighting to hold back the tears, holding on to him like a lost child. "Yes, yes —tomorrow, Joe—we can get the papers. Don't ever go away from me, Joe. Oh, I'm afraid."

"Don't be, don't be."

"I can't help it. I'm afraid tomorrow ——"

He put a finger to her lips. "Tomorrow we'll get a license. Then we'll be married. I've never wanted to stop before. But I do now, more than anything on earth. And I will."

The drive back into town was very quiet.

It was late when he returned to his room. He hated to return. If there were only something they could *do,* some place to go *now,* while he knew he could! But there was nothing to do until tomorrow, and he was cold with fear. He walked into the room and snapped on the lights.

His eyes fell on the blue canvas bag.

It was old and worn and very dusty. The dust from a thousand long roads of a thousand countries was ground into it, and it seemed to be alive, a living thing with a power of its own worn deep into its dusty folds. An ordinary old-fashioned bag, really; over the years he had grown to like it with a strange fondness. It was his home, his only real connection with the world through which he had been drifting like a ghost. A good strong friend, always there, carrying the few things he owned. He had walked miles, once, to get it back when it had been left behind.

And now he hated it.

Even as he looked at it, the drums were beating in his ears again—his own heartbeat? He didn't know. He stared at the bag, and ghosts began to wander through his mind. The miles had been long and dusty, but they had been free miles. He had been lonely, very lonely, but always, he had been free. And now. . . .

He took the bag up on his lap and opened it. Inside, there

were odds and ends. An old pack of cigarettes and an ancient straight-razor. A couple of unused bullets, a pair of stick-on rubber soles for his shoes, a shabby torn handkerchief. Like a strong wind the memories flowed through his mind, the call of the road, the long dark nights under the glistening star blanket. And now he would stop, throw away the bag, settle down in a house, get a job to go to every day. . . . Once stopped, he could never drift again.

The coldness grew deeper. Nervously he dropped the bag on the floor, kicked it across the room. It was nonsense to think that way. He hated the road and all the loneliness it had meant. He *wouldn't* go back, not with a girl like Jeannie to keep him from ever being lonely again.

The chill grew into fear. He sat down on the bed, trembling. He was afraid. He was fighting now, and a voice was whispering in his ear, *You've got to go, Joe, you can't stop, never, never—run now, before you hurt her any more! You can never stop drifting, Joe.*

He gripped the bed until his fingers turned white. He searched his memory, trying to think back, trying to remember how it had started, so long ago. It was as though a great hand were pushing him, drawing him toward the canvas bag, urging him to pack it up, take it and race away, like the wind, onto the road again. But he didn't want to go, he wanted a wife, a home.

Home, Joe? You hated your home!

No, no, he thought. A line of sweat was standing out on his upper lip. I didn't hate it, I was young, I didn't understand, I didn't know.

You threw a curse on your home, Joe. Remember? You screamed it in your mother's face, you swore at her and packed your canvas bag.

I didn't know what I was doing, he thought. I was foolish. I couldn't have known.

But you said it, Joe. Remember what you said?

No!

I'll never come home if I live a thousand years.

He grabbed at the bag. His hand closed on the handle, and he felt it start tugging at him. He let out a cry, and threw it on the floor. Wildly he jerked the telephone from the hook, dialed Jeannie's number, and heard her sleepy voice.

"Jeannie, you've got to help me," he choked. "Come over, please, I can't help myself."

There had been other times he'd tried. He remembered them, now, horrible struggles that had nearly killed him until he gave up. He had never believed in ghosts and witches and curses, but something was forcing him now, something within him so cold, so dark and powerful that he could never hope to fight it. He sat on the edge of the bed, grinding his teeth together, and the voice was crying louder and louder, *You can never stop, Joe, no matter what happens, you'll never have a home again, never, never, never.*

The room was empty when she arrived. She choked back a sob, closed the door behind her, and leaned against the wall. She was too late. The dresser drawers were ripped open; a dirty sock lay under the bed. He was gone, and so was the canvas bag.

Her eye fell on a folded white paper on the floor. She picked it up with trembling fingers, and saw what it was. With a little cry she put it into her pocket, and ran down the front stairs, her coat flying behind her.

The street was dark and empty. A light shone across the street, and another, up near the end of town, made a sad yellow patch in the darkness. She ran faster, her heels snapping on the dry sidewalk, until she turned into a lighted building at the end of the street.

A sleepy clerk looked up at her and blinked.

"Was—was a young man in here?"

The clerk nodded, frowning. "Bus to Chicago. Getting ready to leave."

She threw her money down, and snatched up the little white ticket. Seconds later she was outside, running toward a large bus with CHICAGO across the front. She stumbled up the steps, and then she saw him.

He was sitting near the back, eyes closed, face deathly white. In his arms he was holding his blue canvas bag, and his whole body was trembling. Slowly she moved back, sank down in the seat beside him. "Oh, Joe, Joe ——"

"Jeannie, I'm sorry, I just can't help it."

"I know, Joe."

He looked at her, his eyes widening. She shook her head, and took his heavy hand in hers. Then he saw the ticket.

"Jeannie ——"

"Hush. Don't say it."

"But you don't know what you're doing! We can never have a home, darling, *never.* No matter how hard we try. Think of the long, homeless roads, Jeannie, all over the world, on and on, maybe even to the stars."

She smiled, nodding gently. "But at least you won't be lonely now."

"Jeannie, you *can't.*"

"I can," she said, and rested her head quietly against his shoulder.

Recall

1. The story happens in (a) a small town (b) a city (c) the country.
2. At the beginning of the story, Jeannie is late because she (a) really doesn't care for Joe (b) talks on the phone too long (c) has to work.
3. Joe is both happy and nervous about (a) telling Jeannie about his past (b) asking Jeannie to marry him (c) asking Jeannie for a loan.
4. Joe takes Jeannie to (a) a cheap dance hall (b) an expensive restaurant (c) a bus station.
5. When Joe asks his big question, Jeannie seems both pleased and (a) totally surprised (b) carefree (c) troubled.
6. Joe is amazed to find he can't remember (a) his age (b) Jeannie's last name (c) his last name.
7. To make Joe aware of his past, Jeannie gives him (a) a calendar (b) the names of places he might have visited (c) a pencil and paper.
8. Joe's past has included (a) fighting in wars (b) dropping out of several colleges (c) being killed three times.
9. Joe discovers that he has drifted for (a) fifty years (b) a hundred years (c) 150 years.
10. According to Jeannie, the really important question is (a) "Why don't you look old?" (b) "Where have you drifted?" (c) "What makes you do it?"
11. After learning the truth about Joe's amazing background, Jeannie (a) still wants to marry Joe (b) asks for time to think it over (c) realizes Joe can become rich.

12. Back in his room, Joe (a) discovers he really doesn't like Jeannie (b) feels forced to leave town (c) decides it would be better to leave town.
13. During the night Joe is bothered by (a) worries about money (b) a voice that whispers in his ear (c) a loud radio in the next room.
14. Jeannie comes to Joe's boarding house because (a) he calls her (b) a little voice tells her to (c) she dreams that Joe is leaving town.
15. The story ends (a) in Joe's room (b) in a diner (c) on a bus.

Infer

16. Twice in the story, Joe kicks the canvas bag. He probably does so because (a) it's in his way in the small room (b) he's angry at Jeannie (c) it reminds him of his unhappy past.
17. Joe is caught between what he wants and (a) what Jeannie wants (b) what he feels forced to do (c) what his small income will pay for.
18. Joe's "inner voice" indicates that he cannot have a home because (a) he once cursed his family's home and left it (b) Jeannie doesn't want a home (c) no other home could equal his mother's.
19. At the end of the story, a very difficult decision is made by (a) Joe (b) Jeannie (c) the clerk in the bus station.
20. We can be fairly sure that (a) Joe will stop drifting (b) Joe will not stop drifting (c) Joe will make Jeannie unhappy.

Vocabulary Review

1. If you come to a police *barrier,* you should (a) feed it dog biscuits (b) not cross it (c) listen with respect.
2. A bell that *tinkles* is usually (a) loud (b) soft (c) cracked.
3. A *drifter* is a person who (a) shovels snow (b) tells the future from cloud formations (c) finds it hard to settle down.
4. Most likely to be made of *canvas* would be (a) an army tent (b) a handkerchief (c) a flag.
5. A *boardinghouse* always (a) is made of boards (b) furnishes free meals (c) has rooms for rent.
6. During a *depression* many people can't find (a) enough goods in stores (b) jobs (c) time to think.

Critical Thinking

1. The title of the story indicates the importance of the canvas bag. Exactly what does it stand for?
2. What does the story say about the life of a drifter? One advantage is mentioned—what is it? What are some of the disadvantages?
3. In several ways, the most interesting person in the story is not Joe, but Jeannie. How is she an unusual person? What makes her interesting?
4. The story illustrates the old saying about a person's words coming back to haunt him or her. What did Joe say that put a curse on his life? Describe a time when you spoke angry words that you later felt sorry about.

5. What does the story say about the values of home? It's easy for a person to curse his home and even to leave it, but what's wrong with doing so?

The Girl Who Lived Twice

Frank Edwards

It's happened more than once: a young child seems to have clear memories of having lived before as another human being! Usually, as the child grows a bit older, the memories fade and finally disappear. Usually too, the child's stories are considered to be no more than "crazy talk." But Shanti Devi's case is different. Her memories grew sharper until her ninth year, and a group of scientists made a complete investigation. See if you can explain the amazing mystery of Shanti Devi.

Vocabulary Preview

CHILDBIRTH (CHILD-burth) the act of giving birth to a child

• With modern medicine, only two out of every thousand mothers die in *childbirth.*

DIALECT (DI-uh-lekt) a way of speaking a certain language

• Southerners and northerners speak different *dialects* of American English.

IMAGINARY (im-MAJ-uh-nair-ee) not real; living only in one's imagination

• A lonely young child may make up an *imaginary* friend to play with and talk to.

SANITY (SAN-uh-tee) mental health; the opposite of *insanity* or *madness*

• Sometimes Margo wondered about her little brother's *sanity.*

YEARNING (YURN-ing) a deep desire for something

• Leah always had a *yearning* to see the Pacific Ocean.

THE YOUNG GIRL CLAIMED THAT SHE HAD lived before . . . and the scientists who put her to the test had to shake their heads in wonder. Hers was a case they could neither explain—nor deny!

The parents of Shanti Devi lived quietly in Delhi, India, where she was born in 1926. There was nothing unusual about her birth—nothing at all that might have warned her parents of what was to follow.

As the little girl began to grow out of her babyhood, her mother noticed that she often seemed confused. She kept to herself and sometimes seemed to be talking to an imaginary person.

It was not until she was seven years old, however, that her parents became worried about her sanity. That was the year that little Shanti told her mother that she had lived before, in a town called Muttra. She even described the house where she claimed to have lived in this earlier life.

Her mother told Shanti's father. He, in turn, took the child to a doctor, who questioned her closely. After the child had told her strange story, the doctor could explain nothing. If the little girl was ill, it was a most unusual illness. And if not, then he dared not guess at the truth. He told the father to question the child from time to time and to write down the answers.

Shanti Devi never changed her story. By the time she was nine years old her parents were not surprised at anything she told them. In truth, they had come to believe that something was definitely wrong with her mind. It was in 1935 that the girl told her parents that she had given birth to three children. She described the youngsters and gave their names. She claimed that her own name in that first life had been Ludgi.

Her parents only smiled and tried to hide their sadness.

One evening while Shanti and her mother were preparing the evening meal, there was a knock at the door. The girl ran to open it. When she failed to return soon, her mother began to wonder what was keeping her. She found Shanti staring at a strange man who stood on the steps. The child said, "Mother! This is the cousin of my husband. He lived in the town of Muttra, too, not far from where we lived!"

The stranger did live in Muttra! He had come to talk business with Shanti's father. He did not recognize Shanti. But he told her parents that he had a cousin whose wife, named Ludgi, had died in childbirth ten years before. The worried parents told him of their daughter's strange story about a former life. He agreed to get his cousin to come to Delhi to see if Shanti could recognize him.

The girl was told nothing of the plan. But when the strange man arrived, she threw herself in his arms and sobbed that he was her husband . . . come back to her. The confused man went with Shanti's parents to the local government office, where they told their amazing story. The government of India appointed a special committee of scientists to check into the case.

Had the dead woman, Ludgi, really come back to life in the body of Shanti Devi?

The scientists took Shanti to the town of Muttra. As she stepped off the train, she pointed out and correctly named the mother and brother of the man she said had been her husband. Soon she was talking to them in the Indian dialect used in Muttra, although the dialect she had learned from her parents was quite different.

The puzzled scientists continued their test. They blindfolded the girl and put her into a carriage, climbing in beside her. She directed the driver through the town, described the different places they passed—and finally ordered him to stop at the end of a narrow street. "This," she said, "is where I lived!" When the bandages were removed from her eyes, she saw an old man who sat smoking in front of the house. "That man was my father-in-law," she told them. And, indeed, he had been the father-in-law of Ludgi!

Oddly, she recognized the two oldest children; but not the youngest, whose birth had cost Ludgi's life.

The scientists were careful in their comments. They agreed that somehow the child born in Delhi seemed to remember a life in Muttra, and to remember it in amazing detail. The scientists reported that they could find nothing that suggested a trick. Neither could they find an explanation for what they had seen.

The full story of Shanti Devi, now living quietly as a government worker in New Delhi, can be found in medical and government reports. In 1958 she told doctors who questioned her that she had learned to live in the present; that the old yearning for her past no longer bothered her.

Shanti Devi is living proof that some things that really happen are stranger than fiction.

Recall

1. Shanti's parents first noticed strange things about her (a) at birth (b) as she grew out of babyhood (c) at age nine.
2. When Shanti first told part of her strange story, her parents (a) believed every word (b) immediately called in a group of scientists (c) thought she might be insane.

3. Ludgi was (a) Shanti's mother (b) the dead woman whose memories Shanti seemed to share (c) the dead woman's husband.
4. When Shanti saw the man she said had been her husband, she (a) rushed into his arms (b) drew back in fright (c) accused him of killing her.
5. Shanti could not recognize Ludgi's youngest child because (a) the child had been in a bad accident (b) Ludgi had died when the child was born (c) the child was a tiny baby when Shanti first saw it.

Infer

6. The scientists probably blindfolded Shanti (a) so she wouldn't be recognized (b) to anger her (c) to check on her description of things they passed.
7. The author's purpose in writing the story was probably to (a) make up a story that sounded true (b) get the facts and tell them as they really happened (c) persuade people that scientists are fools.
8. Nothing in the story suggests that (a) Shanti was trying to fool people (b) the scientists were puzzled (c) Shanti's reports were accurate.
9. If we accept this strange story as true, we have to admit that (a) ghosts are real (b) all people have lived former lives (c) there are some things science cannot explain.
10. Another good title might be (a) "Living with Ludgi" (b) "The Double Life of Shanti Devi" (c) "Life in India."

Vocabulary Review

1. In hygiene class, we saw a movie about *childbirth. Childbirth* means (a) the act of carrying a child (b) the act of giving birth (c) teenage mothers.
2. From the woman's *dialect,* I felt sure she came from the Boston area. The word *dialect* refers to (a) clothing (b) manners (c) speech.
3. People who are scared by *imaginary* dangers often show courage in the face of real dangers. *Imaginary* means (a) real (b) unreal (c) strange.
4. After the ninth-inning home run had won the game, everyone in the ball park seemed to lose his *sanity.* In this sentence, *sanity* refers to (a) cleanliness (b) good sense (c) money.
5. Julio has a *yearning* for pistachio ice cream. *Yearning* means (a) hatred (b) bowl (c) desire.

Critical Thinking

1. "The Girl Who Lived Twice" is a fascinating tale because it really does seem to be true. Look back at the story now to find reasons why someone might believe it to be true. For instance, what is the importance of the age at which Shanti Devi first began acting strange? What is the importance of Ludgi's husband's cousin arriving at Shanti's house almost by accident? Try to find other reasons.

2. What were the tests the scientists gave Shanti? What is another test they might have given but didn't?
3. What is the best explanation you can think of for the puzzle of Shanti Devi? Your explanation can be a supernatural one, or you can think of a way Shanti might have fooled people.
4. Do you know the word *reincarnation*? If not, look it up. Explain how it might apply to the story of Shanti Devi.

The Devil in Devonshire

John Godwin

When one person says that he's seen something impossible happen, we might say he's crazy. When a small group of people announce that they've witnessed the impossible, we might look for a plot or a secret plan. But when thousands of people agree that the impossible has, in fact, really taken place, we probably wouldn't know what to say. We're puzzled and even angered by what our minds cannot explain. So it is when we read of the strange happenings that occurred over a hundred years ago in Devonshire, on the south coast of England. The events remain a mystery; their cause remains unknown.

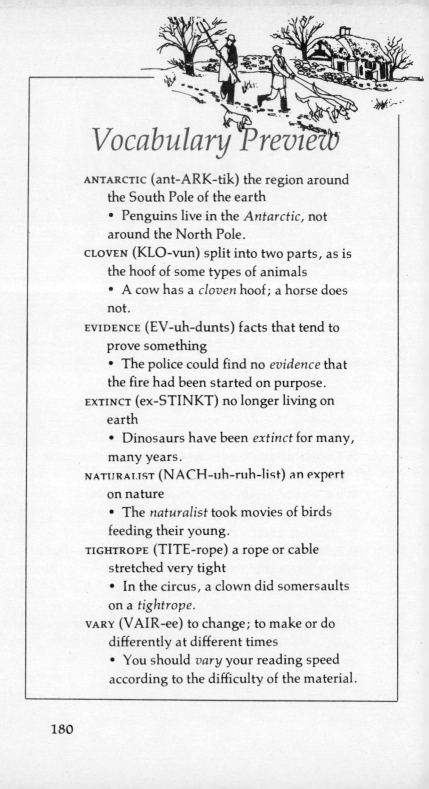

Vocabulary Preview

ANTARCTIC (ant-ARK-tik) the region around the South Pole of the earth

• Penguins live in the *Antarctic,* not around the North Pole.

CLOVEN (KLO-vun) split into two parts, as is the hoof of some types of animals

• A cow has a *cloven* hoof; a horse does not.

EVIDENCE (EV-uh-dunts) facts that tend to prove something

• The police could find no *evidence* that the fire had been started on purpose.

EXTINCT (ex-STINKT) no longer living on earth

• Dinosaurs have been *extinct* for many, many years.

NATURALIST (NACH-uh-ruh-list) an expert on nature

• The *naturalist* took movies of birds feeding their young.

TIGHTROPE (TITE-rope) a rope or cable stretched very tight

• In the circus, a clown did somersaults on a *tightrope.*

VARY (VAIR-ee) to change; to make or do differently at different times

• You should *vary* your reading speed according to the difficulty of the material.

THROUGHOUT THAT GRAY AFTERNOON OF February 8, 1855, the area around the town of Topsham in southwestern England looked like a hunting ground. Women, children, and old folks remained hidden indoors, while the country was alive with men and dogs. Shotguns, pistols, pitchforks, and clubs were everywhere in sight.

The men were walking back and forth and in circles through the thick snow, peering behind bushes, poking into farmyards, orchards, and cemeteries. Some of the hunters thought they might find a mysterious animal of strange shape, about the size of a donkey. The rest, however, thought they were looking for *THE DEVIL.*

The belief that the Devil was walking around nearby caused folks that frightened easily to stay in their houses and lock the doors. The braver ones grabbed whatever weapons they owned and went after the Evil One—though not quite sure just what they would do if they found him. Most people had no doubt that he was pretty close at hand—for the marks of his cloven hooves were easily seen in the snow.

The people who went on this hunt were not ignorant or backward. They were not the kind of people who believed in witches and saw devils everywhere. They had simply been frightened out of their wits by a happening that would leave the greatest scientists of the country as puzzled as the local citizens.

A century ago, the county of Devonshire—proudly called "Glorious Devon"—was known as one of the prettiest and happiest sections of England. Famous for its apple cider and beautiful coast, Devon was the home of practical, quiet, hard-working people. Here was the last place one would expect to find people frightened by a devil, either real or imaginary.

On the night of February 7, a heavy snow covered the southern part of the country. The flakes began to fall around eight o'clock, and the fall continued until close to midnight. By then nearly everyone in the country was asleep.

About six the following morning, Henry Pilk, a baker, stepped out of his backyard bakehouse in the small town of Topsham. The yard and the street beyond were covered by a white layer of snow, as smooth as a fresh bedsheet. Or almost so. For as Mr. Pilk looked at the snow, he noticed a line of the strangest footprints he had ever seen.

Each print was shaped like a small horseshoe. At first, the baker thought they might have been made by a pony. But then he saw that each print was in line—*each in front of the other*—and therefore, more like the tracks of a two-footed than a four-footed animal.

Surprisingly, the prints started at a wooden six-foot fence, came close to the bakehouse, and then went off toward the fence again. Mr. Pilk took note of the tracks, then went about his work. He did not trouble to look over his fence, nor did he search his brain for the kind of animal that had visited his yard during the night.

An hour later, his yard was visited by a group of neighbors which included Albert Brailford, a schoolteacher. The group had followed the tracks from the street, hoping to catch sight of whatever had left them. Pilk joined them. Together, they trailed the prints back onto the street.

The group swelled rapidly: women, children, shopkeepers—running up from all directions. As they went on and word of the hunt spread, citizens called out again and again, announcing newly found evidence. To everyone's growing surprise, it was learned that the same hoofmarks were outside almost every house on the street, and also in the fields beyond. People waved excitedly from garden gates and doorways: "Over here—they're here, too!"

Now the entire town was buzzing with the news. As more and more people spilled out their stories, it became clear that Topsham had been visited by some strange creature with frightening powers: a creature that could walk through walls!

For some of the tracks led into gardens surrounded by stone walls 12 feet high. The gates were locked; the snow on top of the walls lay undisturbed. *Yet the single line of prints advanced straight at the walls and continued on the other side, as if nothing had been in its path.*

The search went on. It now turned out that almost every house in town had been visited by the strange creature. The trail ran mostly along the ground. But sometimes the trail jumped up onto roofs, and even over snow-covered wagons which had been left standing overnight. The tracks never doubled back. They went on, passing each point only once, zig-zagging right and left as if the strange visitor had looked into every house.

And while the citizens of Topsham were looking through their streets, the people of other towns were doing the same. For the mysterious prints were discovered along almost 100 miles of the south Devon coast!

Topsham, located on the Exe River, marked the northern tip of the "printed" region. Totnes, about 97 miles down the coast, was the southern tip. Between these points, almost every town and village—and yes! even lonely farms—awoke to find the hoofmarks on doorsteps and roofs. They were discovered along lonely beaches, in stretches of woodland, on main streets, in market squares. All of these prints must have been made during the past night. But no one in the area could remember either seeing or hearing anything that might be a clue to their maker.

The reports grew stranger by the hour. At Mamhead, a local doctor named Benson followed a line of the prints across an open field. They stopped at an 18-foot haystack which was covered with snow. The snow on the haystack was unmarked—but the tracks continued on the other side. It was as if whatever had caused them had simply stepped over the huge haystack in its path.

Near the same town, two hunters spent a couple of hours following the hoofmarks through thick and thorny bushes. If an animal had passed this way, bits of its fur or hair probably would have caught on the thorny bushes. But the two men found no signs of anything. They found only the mysterious tracks, which stopped suddenly at one point, as though the creature had flown off. But half a mile further in the same direction, they sighted them again—this time on the roofs of a row of cottages. From this height, the tracks came back to earth, and then went on—in a straight line—until they reached the streets of Mamhead.

Nothing, it seemed, had stopped the unknown creature. Between Powderham and Lympstone lay the mouth of the Exe River, unfrozen, and almost two miles wide. Yet the trail led up to the western bank of the river and continued on the other side. It started right at the water's edge, as if the thing had either swum or stepped across. The same had happened at other rivers and streams along the way.

The prints were easy enough to follow, since they looked like no other marks left in the snow. They stuck out like signposts. Before they gradually faded away, several hundred people, up and down the coast, had made drawings of them. The shape of the drawings varied slightly. But the outline and size were nearly the same, and looked like this:

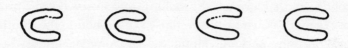

The hoofmarks looked like those of a donkey. They measured four inches by two and one-half inches. The distance between each print—that is, the length of the creature's step or stride—was always eight inches. This was true whether the trail lay across level ground, through thick woods, or over rooftops. By itself this was a very odd fact, since animals, like humans, vary their strides to suit where they are walking.

But even more puzzling was the straight single line of the prints. Every four-footed animal moves by placing its feet right and left, leaving a clear double track. Even two-footed creatures, like birds and humans, do not place one foot *exactly* in front of the other, unless walking a tightrope. But this was exactly what the thing seemed to have been doing—walking along some invisible single line that stretched in zigzag fashion from Totnes to Topsham.

The first reaction to the happening was simply curiosity. As long as the prints were fresh and undisturbed, the local people enjoyed the exciting game of discovery and guesswork. Everyone put in his or her opinion. In time, it was agreed, scientists would come up with a good explanation.

But as the day wore on and the tracks began to blur, the excitement gave way to worry, and finally to fear. The blurring caused changes in some of the marks. A rumor began that the tracks were those of a *cloven hoof* (which they were not). The Devil, as everyone knew, had such hooves. The

Devil also might have been able to walk through walls and step over rivers. The news spread by word of mouth, from village to village, that last night the Devil had wandered around south Devonshire, looking into every house, probably to mark down future victims. Within hours, the hunting game became serious. Hundreds of volunteers took their hunting dogs and proceeded to search the countryside, quite ready to tackle the Evil One.

By late afternoon, the tracks had disappeared. But the countryside was still filled with armed search parties, men on horseback, and barking dogs. Rumors spread faster than the prints faded. Some folks swore they had seen the hoofmarks glowing like live coals in the snow. Others had heard devilish laughter echoing through lonely forests. Still others had seen a huge shadow over Powderham Castle. The most widespread story was that the prints disappeared before your eyes when you looked at them. They reappeared magically the moment you turned your back.

People dreaded the coming of darkness. Most thought that IT was sure to return in the night to . . . well, no one knew just what. Having failed to find anything, the members of the search parties went to their houses and stayed there. The inns were empty. Few dared risk a walk home after dark. But nearly every house and cottage kept its lamps or its candles burning.

Nothing happened that night. The next day what disturbed people most was the confusion of the "experts." England has always been full of naturalists. It is a country whose newspapers have pages and pages of letters about the habits of frogs, and the exact date and place of the year's first cuckoo call. As a group, these naturalists had a great deal of knowledge of animals. All of it was used to try to explain the mysterious hoofprints. But the result was a huge zero.

The simplest ideas—that the footprints were made by a donkey, or a pony, or a horse—were thrown out immediately. Everyone was familiar with the tracks of these animals. Then some people thought the tracks might have been made by one of the less common creatures, such as a deer, a beaver, or a fox. This idea also was discarded. Neither the prints nor the method of walking of these animals was like the tracks. There simply wasn't any four-footer that could have left a single trail.

A bird, of course, would have been able to get over things like garden walls and to fly across rivers. But who had ever heard of a hoofed bird? A hoofed bird that could walk a single line for 97 miles?

The pattern of the prints confused people even more than the prints themselves. All animals have a reason for their moves. Usually, the animal is in search of food. This trail, however, ruled out any kind of food gathering. The trail showed a steady forward progress without any wayside stops for feeding.

Having drawn a blank with every kind of living thing, the guessers finally turned to nonliving things. Yes, there was something about the trail that indicated a machine rather than a walking creature. The single line, the regular eight-inch space between each mark, the clearness of every print, certainly did suggest some sort of machine. It could have been rolled over the countryside by someone with no other purpose than to fool people.

The possibility of a joke was, therefore, considered quite seriously. It would not have been too hard to build a gadget that would leave those hoofmarks in the snow. Perhaps a wheel with hoofs attached eight inches apart, that could be rolled along the ground. Or better yet, a print marker that fitted over the joker's own shoes!

But these suggestions were soon seen to be impossible. For the maker of such a machine would have had only about six hours of darkness in which to do his work. He would have had to finish before six in the morning. To cover the whole 97-mile area, he would have had to move at the rate of more than 16 miles per hour. And he'd have to get over walls and rivers—an impossibility for any human.

What about several people—a whole group of jokers working together? Even that idea did not stand up. How would such people have jumped across garden walls without disturbing the snow on top? How would they have leapt over haystacks and have walked over sloping roofs? And why—if they had used anything besides their feet—were there no tell-tale tracks, except those hoofmarks?

At first, only southern Devonshire was excited by these questions. But soon, most of England joined in. Several London newspapers printed the story, resulting in an immediate flow of visitors to Devonshire. Some came with big rifles; others with drawing books and magnifying glasses. All were eager to see the mysterious beast or at least its tracks. All were disappointed. There was plenty of snow during the days that followed, but the prints never did reappear.

The guessing game was now in full swing. Newspapers printed many letters on the subject. There was barely a beast or bird, alive or extinct, which was not mentioned by some letter writer. The list read alphabetically from auk to zebra. In between, there were giant leaping rats, huge rabbits, bears walking upright, escaped circus camels, and even penguins. None of the letter writers offered any idea as to what might have become of the animal *after* it had finished its night walk.

Most of the letters weren't really worth printing. But the wide interest did bring some interesting guesses. An English teacher at Heidelberg University wrote to the *London Illustrated News* that he had discussed the puzzle with a Russian. The Russian had told him that similar prints had appeared several times in an area in Poland. The local farmers wouldn't follow them or even go near them, since they belonged to some unknown creature.

Another reader drew attention to an account left by the Antarctic explorer, Sir James Ross, some 15 years earlier. In May, 1840, Captain Ross's ship visited Kerguelen Island, an unfriendly, rocky place near the Antarctic Circle. The men who went on shore came across "strange footsteps belonging to a donkey or a pony." The search group tried to follow them, only to lose sight of the prints on rocky ground. According to Ross, the marks were "three inches in length and two and a half in breadth, and the shape of a horseshoe."

Kerguelen, now an island owned by France, has been thoroughly explored. But no beast that might have left such hoofprints has been seen there. In fact, there is no animal known that would leave such hoofmarks.

The "devil's hoofmarks" never again appeared in Devonshire, nor in any part of England. Nobody so far has been able to show even the smallest of links between the odd hoofprints found in Poland, those found on the edge of the Antarctic, and those seen in southern England. Perhaps there is no such link.

Recall

1. The prints were first noticed (a) about midnight, when it stopped snowing (b) early in the morning (c) just before the snow melted.
2. One strange thing about the prints was that they were (a) exactly in front of each other (b) nearly four feet apart (c) the same depth in the snow.
3. The prints were always (a) nearly round (b) the same distance apart (c) like those of a four-footed animal.
4. The creature seemed to jump over walls and haystacks, but it did step on (a) wagons (b) trees (c) roofs.
5. Zig-zagging here and there, the prints covered a distance of about (a) 10 miles (b) 100 miles (c) 1,000 miles.
6. At first, the people looked at the prints with (a) great curiosity (b) fear (c) thoughts of the Devil.
7. Talk of the Devil started about the time (a) it was discovered that the prints went from house to house (b) the prints began to blur (c) everyone saw the prints disappear and reappear.
8. The hunt for the Devil was conducted (a) as a joke by most people (b) very seriously (c) to please a few worried old people.
9. By early evening Devonshire was filled with (a) the Devil's footprints (b) rumors of the Devil (c) visitors from other parts of England.
10. The author makes it clear that the prints were not, in fact, (a) cloven (b) clear at first (c) regularly in line.
11. In the days that followed, interest in the strange prints was stirred up by (a) a baker named Henry Pilk (b) radio and television (c) newspapers.
12. The idea that an animal might have made the prints was discarded because (a) there were few animals in Devon-

shire (b) Devonshire donkeys didn't wear horseshoes (c) no known animal walked in that manner.

13. Also discarded was the idea that the prints had been made by (a) creatures from Mars (b) a machine of some kind (c) ice dropped from the sky.

14. The author states that similar prints have (a) never been noted anywhere else (b) been proven to exist in two other places (c) been reported elsewhere.

15. The author also refers to the Devil as (a) the Prince of Darkness (b) Satan (c) the Evil One.

Infer

16. "Between Powderham and Lympstone lay the mouth of the Exe River, unfrozen, and almost two miles wide." In this sentence, *mouth* means (a) noise (b) source or beginning (c) end which is near the sea.

17. The selection illustrates the amazing power of (a) rumors (b) human intelligence (c) people armed with weapons.

18. It appears to be a fact that (a) the Devil walked in Devonshire (b) the tracks were made by some machine (c) mysterious footprints were found in the snow.

19. The author suggests that the prints were probably caused by (a) one of the animals mentioned (b) something that still remains unknown (c) a group of jokers.

20. Another good title for this selection might be (a) "The Donkey in Devonshire" (b) "Animal, Vegetable, or Mineral?" (c) "The Mysterious Footprints."

Vocabulary Review

On your paper, write the *italicized* word that best fills the blank in each sentence.

Antarctic	*evidence*	*naturalist*	*vary*
cloven	*extinct*	*tightrope*	

1. An American bird that once numbered in the millions, the passenger pigeon is now ———.
2. Polar bears live in the northern hemisphere, not in the ———.
3. The deer's small ——— hoofs left tracks in the snow.
4. Several people have walked on a ——— stretched across Niagara Falls.
5. The ——— was an expert on the insects of the Southwest.
6. Running long distances is easier if you ——— your speed now and then.
7. Both the bullet and the gun were produced as ——— in the courtroom.

Critical Thinking

1. For what reasons was it decided that the tracks could not have been made by an animal? Why did it seem impossible that they could have been made by a machine of some kind?

2. Describe the changing reactions of the people of Devonshire to the mysterious footprints as the day went on. What do you think accounted for these changes?

3. If the footprints had been found in your locality last year, how do you think people would have reacted? How would these reactions be different from those of the Devonshire people in 1855?

4. To this day, the cause of the "Devil's footprints" is a mystery. Try to think up an explanation of your own that is not mentioned in the account by John Godwin.

The Great Amherst Mystery

Walter Hubbell

Of all the mysteries of the unseen world, the most amazing—because the most common!—is probably the poltergeist. What are poltergeists? Some people call them "ghosts." Other people, trying to be scientific, call them "unexplained forces." At any rate, poltergeists are "ghosts" or "forces" that haunt houses, usually by making strange rapping noises, moving furniture, and throwing small objects from place to place. Over the years, several investigations of poltergeists have revealed an interesting fact: they seem to trouble only households that contain a teenager, nearly always a girl. Here, in shortened form, is Walter Hubbell's account of the strange events that surrounded a young woman named Esther Cox.

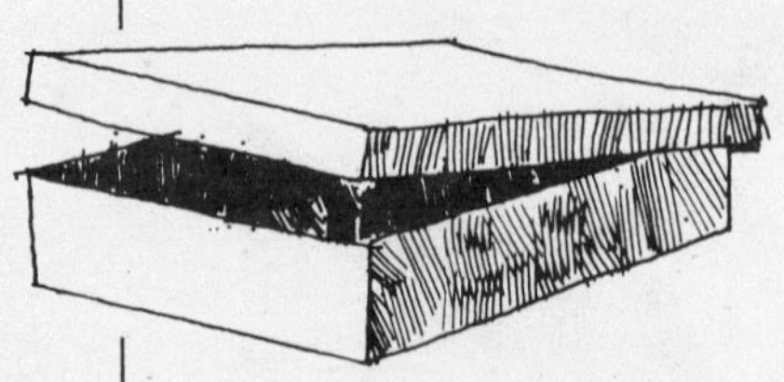

Vocabulary Preview

AVOCATION (av-uh-KAY-shun) a hobby; a leisure-time activity

• Donna's *avocation* is painting pictures.

DECEPTION (dee-SEP-shun) trickery; action that fools another person

• Good magicians are experts at *deception*.

EXPOSED (ek-SPOZED) uncovered; revealed the truth about

• Senator Hurlburt said he had *exposed* the governor's "secret deals."

FRAUD (FRAWD) dishonesty; conduct that cheats another person

• But the senator failed to produce proof of any *fraud*.

JOURNAL (JUR-nul) a professional magazine

• The old doctor no longer read medical *journals*.

VOCATION (vo-KAY-shun) a profession; a career activity

• Every young person should choose at least a few courses in school which will be helpful to the *vocation* he or she works at later in life.

IT'S A STRANGE WORLD, THIS ONE WE LIVE in. I don't believe in ghosts. That is, I didn't believe in ghosts before I investigated the mystery of Esther Cox. Now the only question is what to call them—ghosts, spirits, poltergeists, or what?

My name is Walter Hubbell. By vocation, I'm an actor. By avocation, I'm an investigator of the "supernatural." During the past few years, I've investigated many people who claimed they could talk to the spirits of the dead. They were all fakes, and I exposed them. As an actor, I know all the tricks that we use on the stage. I also know most of the tricks that magicians use to fool the public. I am, beyond doubt, able to judge whether or not deception was used in the case of Esther Cox. And it was not.

Truth is often stranger than fiction. What I have written here is truth—not fiction—and it is *very strange.*

I was acting in Canada when I first heard of Esther Cox. She was nineteen years old at the time. She and her sister Jennie, age twenty-two, lived in the home of an older married sister, Olive Teed. Daniel Teed, Olive's husband, was a foreman in a shoe factory. The Teeds had two small boys. Before the trouble started, all lived together in a rented house in the town of Amherst.

Then things started to happen. One night Esther thought she heard a mouse somewhere in her bed. She awakened her sister Jennie, who slept in the same room. They listened in silence, and soon went back to sleep. But the next night, both sisters heard the noise again, louder than ever. "It's in that box, under my bed," declared Esther. Together the two sisters pulled the green cardboard box out from under the bed. It jumped, and both girls screamed. Jennie slowly took hold of the box and placed it in the middle of the room. It jumped again, rising a foot in the air and falling back on its side. The girls' screams brought Daniel Teed hurrying into the room. He listened to their story. "You're both crazy," he announced, shaking his head as he kicked the box back under the bed. "Now go to sleep and don't disturb me again!"

This was just the beginning. A few nights later, another scream echoed through the house. It was Esther: "What's happening to me? I'm swelling up! I'm going to burst!" This time the whole family ran to the bedroom, and there was Esther, confused and worried, her whole body swollen beyond belief. What had happened? What could they do? Daniel Teed was about to call a doctor, when, quite suddenly, came a loud rapping noise, as if someone were pounding with a heavy hammer on the floor under Esther's bed. The swelling started to go down. The rapping continued, and Esther looked more comfortable. Soon she fell into a tired, troubled sleep.

The next morning Daniel Teed hurried to the family doctor. Dr. Thomas W. Carritte listened patiently, but he didn't believe a word. "I'll come this evening, and I'll stay through the night if I have to," he told Daniel. "But I guarantee you, none of this nonsense is going to happen while *I'm* in the house."

The doctor couldn't have been more wrong. After supper that evening, as he sat in Esther's room, he watched in wonder as an unseen hand seemed to slide the pillow out from under her head. A sheet and a light blanket were pulled from her bed. She began to swell up. Now the doctor had a job to do—but it was not he who cured Esther. It was, again, the loud rapping noises.

Dr. Carritte was as puzzled as everyone else. He knew the family, and he felt sure that no one was trying to fool him. As the rapping went on, he walked outside the house to see if he could discover what caused the noise. From outside the rapping sounded louder, like someone pounding on the roof. But there was no one—on the roof, in the yard, or anywhere.

Not long after, my acting job in Canada having ended, I arrived at the troubled house myself. At the time, I did not believe in ghosts, poltergeists, or spirits of any kind. I did believe that everything that happens has an explanation. From what I'd heard about Esther Cox, it didn't seem likely that she was playing tricks on people. But still, there had to be an explanation. Fortunately, I was able to rent a room from the Teeds, to be nearer the mystery I had come to investigate.

Esther Cox was a short, stout girl who could only be described as plain (her sister Jennie was the pretty one). Though far from dumb, she was not overly intelligent. She certainly didn't understand what was going on. Neither, I was soon persuaded, could she have planned it.

After I'd rented the room, I hadn't been in the house five minutes when my umbrella suddenly seemed to come to life. It flew across the living room. Soon after, Esther appeared in the kitchen doorway, carrying a plate. From behind her, something came flashing through the air—a large knife. It narrowly missed me. I rushed into the kitchen to see who had thrown it. That was my first introduction to ghosts. There was no one there.

"It looks like they don't like you," said Esther.

By "they," it turned out, Esther meant two poltergeists (or *ghosts,* as she called them). One she called "Maggie," the other "Bob." She claimed sometimes that she could see them. Once, as Olive Teed and I looked on in amazement, Esther stared at the thin air in the middle of the living room and told us that Maggie was standing there. Even more strange, the girl swore that Maggie was wearing a pair of black and white socks that belonged to Esther. Feeling a little foolish, I shouted, "Now Maggie, take off Esther's socks—and be quick about it!" A minute later, a pair of black and white socks appeared from out of nowhere. They dropped from the air in front of us to the floor.

After that I stopped looking for explanations. The only explanation was . . . the supernatural.

Whoever—or whatever—"Maggie" and "Bob" were, they seemed to be always in action. With my own eyes, I saw a heavy ash tray leave its place on a table and come whizzing at me, crashing into the wall as I ducked. Furniture constantly slid around the floors. As I entered the dining room one time, every chair fell over with a crash. Another time, needing a light for my pipe, I remarked, "Bob, give me a few matches, if you please." Immediately, a lighted match fell out of the air.

But the poltergeists were not always so helpful. As the weeks passed, Esther's spells continued, and even grew worse. Sometimes she would lie on her bed as if dead, her body swelling up like a balloon, and then collapsing, over and over. Also, the poltergeists were ruining the furniture and damaging the walls. When they started lighting small fires, the Teeds were asked to move. The owner of the house had risked enough. The Teeds were good people, but they would have to go.

As an experiment, the Teeds decided to see what would happen if only Esther left. She was sent to live with a family named Van Amburgh on a farm in the country. And here the affair came to an end with the biggest mystery of all. With Esther out of the house, everything returned to normal. The rappings, the flying objects, the sliding furniture, the fires—all stopped at once.

And perhaps even more strangely, Esther's life in her new home was completely untroubled. Like all poltergeists,

"Maggie" and "Bob" had departed as mysteriously as they had come.

It must be stated that the Teeds made no attempt to keep the strange events secret. Dr. Carritte and others were constantly in and out of the house. I have a statement signed by sixteen persons who witnessed at least some of the happenings I've described. I have a letter from Olive Teed declaring that *all* I've written here is true. And Dr. Carritte writes:

"I take pen in hand to say that what Mr. Walter Hubbell has written about the mysterious Esther Cox is entirely correct. The young lady was a patient of mine both previous to and during those wonderful demonstrations. I tried various experiments, but with no satisfactory results. Honestly doubtful persons were on all occasions soon convinced that there was no fraud or deception in the case. Were I to publish the case in medical journals, as you suggest, I doubt if it would be believed by doctors generally. I am certain I could not have believed such miracles had I not witnessed them."

Recall

1. The author, Walter Hubbell, earned his living (a) acting on the stage (b) investigating poltergeists (c) writing books and articles.
2. The trouble started in the house with (a) strange noises under Esther Cox's bed (b) small objects flying through the air (c) loud rappings on the roof.
3. Esther's troubles included (a) loss of appetite (b) thinking in English but speaking a strange foreign language (c) mysterious swelling of her body.

4. "Maggie" and "Bob" were (a) the Teed children (b) ghosts of dead relatives (c) Esther's names for the poltergeists.
5. According to the author, the activities of the poltergeists were witnessed (a) only by Esther (b) only by himself and Esther (c) by at least sixteen people.
6. The strange activities stopped when (a) Esther moved out of the house (b) Dr. Carritte came to observe (c) Esther ran out of tricks to play.

Infer

7. It is reasonable to suppose that Esther (a) liked the poltergeists because they made her body swell up (b) completely understood all that was happening (c) was troubled by the poltergeists and wished they would go away.
8. The attitudes of both the author and Dr. Carritte changed from (a) anger to approval (b) interest to boredom (c) doubt to belief.
9. The author devotes a good bit of attention to Dr. Carritte, probably because (a) he wants to show how easily doctors can be fooled (b) as a medical man, Dr. Carritte will be respected by most readers (c) he has no other witnesses that his story is true.
10. The author seems most interested in (a) solving the mystery (b) persuading the reader that the strange events really happened (c) showing that it is bad to live with relatives.

Vocabulary Review

On your paper, write the *italicized* word (or words) called for by each of the following questions.

avocation	*expose*	*journal*
deception	*fraud*	*vocation*

1. What two words are nearly opposites?
2. Which of the two words you chose to answer 1 means almost the same thing as "career"?
3. What two words mean nearly the same thing?
4. Which of the two words you chose to answer 3 would you use to describe a magic trick?
5. What word means "to uncover"?
6. What word names something to read?

Critical Thinking

1. What does this old saying mean: "Truth is . . . stranger than fiction"? How does it apply to the story of Esther Cox?
2. There are at least three ways of viewing the story of Esther Cox: (a) Walter Hubbell made the whole thing up; (b) Walter Hubbell told the truth as he saw it, but Esther, probably working with a magician, fooled him; and (c) everything in the story really happened. Which of these three views do you think is nearest the truth? Explain why.
3. Another explanation of the story is that several people, certainly including the Teeds and perhaps Walter Hubbell himself, cooperated with Esther in a plan to fool the public. It

might even be that many people were in on the plan—Esther, Jennie, the Teeds, Hubbell, Dr. Carritte, and perhaps even the sixteen witnesses to "some" of the strange happenings. Which do you prefer, this explanation or the story as Hubbell tells it? Explain.

4. "Poltergeist cases" occur every few years in the United States. Usually they involve mysterious rappings, flying objects, and sliding furniture. The cases are often investigated, and usually no "natural" explanation can be found. Sometimes this explanation is offered:

Poltergeist activity usually happens in homes containing at least one person between eleven and nineteen years of age. As is well known, young people have a lot of energy, both mental and physical. When this energy can't be used or released in some way, it builds up inside the person. In some cases, it builds up enough to suddenly break out with a force that can send a glass flying across a room, tip over a chair, or rap on a wall.

Would you accept this explanation if you investigated a poltergeist case yourself and could find no "natural" causes for the disturbances? Why, or why not?

Watery Poltergeists

Raymond Bayless

What would you do? You're sitting quietly at home one evening. Suddenly you hear a little hiss, then a pop like a firecracker. Where did that come from? While you're wondering, a stream of water squirts out of the wall. You rush to the wall, notice that it's damp, but can find no hole. Then, from another room, you hear a pop and the splatter of water. Soon it's happening in every room in the house. What would you do?

If you live in an apartment, you'd probably call the landlord. Soon perhaps, the Police and Fire Departments would be called in. And if they could find no solution, you might get in touch with someone like Raymond Bayless, an expert on supernatural events. Pay close attention to his step-by-step report on a real "water ghost."

Vocabulary Preview

INSULATION (in-suh-LAY-shun) material placed in the walls and ceiling of a house to prevent the loss or entrance of heat
• *Insulation* keeps a house warmer in winter and cooler in summer.

PANTRY (PAN-tree) a storage room for food and kitchen supplies
• Many old houses have a small *pantry* next to the kitchen.

REPRESENTATIVE (rep-ruh-ZEN-tuh-tiv) a person who represents, or stands for, another person or an organization
• A *representative* of the Student Council will attend the next School Board meeting.

SPIRITUAL (SPEER-ich-wul) religious; having to do with a person's spirit
• Mrs. Wright gave a half hour every morning to prayer and other *spiritual* activities.

VERSION (VUR-zhun) one particular form of a story, article, book, or play
• Which *version* of the story did you hear?

A RATHER RARE EFFECT FOUND WITH poltergeists is the mysterious appearance of water. The amount of liquid may be a few drops, or a near-flood. A very remarkable case was the strange appearance of water at an apartment in Lawrence and a home in Methuen, Massachusetts. Here is a shortened version of the first report that appeared in a Lawrence paper on November 2, 1963.

> Water from an unknown source is practically chasing the Y----- family of nearby Methuen from place to place.
>
> Last Tuesday the family noticed a wet spot on the wall of their TV room. A few moments later they heard a pop, like a firecracker, and water squirted from the wall. This continued until Friday, when there was so much water in the house that the family had to leave it for the night. They moved to the apartment of Mrs. Y-----'s parents, Mr. and Mrs. A-----, here in Lawrence. Saturday morning the strange events began all over again in the apartment.
>
> Five people have seen the odd happenings in the Lawrence apartment.
>
> A crew of Lawrence firemen, two of them with building experience, were asked to check the roof of the three-story apartment house for leaks. They also crawled into the small space between the ceiling of the top apartment and the roof.

The men report the roof is excellent. There is no sign of water or a leak in the space under the roof. Lights flashed down the wall from the roof fail to show a trace of water.

Neither the first-floor nor third-floor apartments are having any trouble, only the apartment of Mr. and Mrs. A----- on the second floor.

A Fire Inspector checked the fact that every squirt from the wall is preceded by a popping noise. He said that there is no hole in the wall afterward. Firemen also said that there were no pipes leaking.

But, strange as things were Saturday at the A-----'s apartment, things were even worse at the Y-----'s house in Methuen.

A representative of a local roofing company called in to test the house in Methuen reports, "There was a quart of water on the sofa. I pulled down a piece of the wall, and it was as dry as a bone." He says that he has never seen anything like it before.

He says the owners tried everything possible to solve the problem.

"They shut off the water and drained the pipes. They shut off the heat and opened windows. They raised all the shades to let in as much sunlight as possible. Nothing seemed to help."

The next newspaper story to describe the strange events bothering the family was published November 4, 1963, and offered several explanations for the mystery. I will give a shortened version of the article and a few direct quotations.

It was stated in the first article that no explanations had been found, but "Now there are enough explanations so you can take your pick."

"The case of the water-squirting walls is officially closed so far as the family, Lawrence police, and the Lawrence and Methuen fire departments are concerned. However, each has its own explanation.

"In a report from the Lawrence police station, investigating officers said that the Y-----'s daughter admitted throwing water on the walls of the apartment of her grandmother (Mrs. A-----). As far as the police are concerned the matter is closed."

However, officials from the Methuen and Lawrence fire departments did not agree with the police explanation. For instance, a Methuen fire official remarked that the girl was helping to "mop up the house when water was exploding in four or five places at once."

"Neither the grandmother nor the parents agree with the police. They claim that the girl never told the police she'd thrown water. They do admit that the girl did spill water in the pantry and break a glass."

After reading these confusing articles, I wrote to an investigating expert and asked for further information. He kindly replied, much as follows:

> This mystery started during the first part of the week in the home of Mr. and Mrs. Y----- and daughter, aged eleven, at their home in Methuen, which is about three miles from here. According to them the condition gradually became worse; so much so that by Friday evening they could no longer occupy the house. They came down to Lawrence and stayed with the wife's parents, Mr. and Mrs. A-----, who live in an apartment.
>
> During the week the Y-----s had an investigator who represented a well-known roofing company. He stayed in the area all week and worked along with the

Y-----s and the Methuen Fire Department to help solve the mystery. There was water everywhere. Mrs. Y----- and her relatives worked on the three floors of their house, mopping up water and attempting to dry out the place. The fire department went so far as to pull down plaster walls, only to find that the wall from which the water came was perfectly dry.

This expert's letter went on to describe the investigation of the A-----'s apartment. More than seven men took part in the investigation and could find nothing wrong with the building. In the next paragraphs of his letter he continued with an interesting happening:

> At one time I was standing in the kitchen of the apartment. I could see part of the pantry. The eleven-year-old girl was in the pantry at the time, but I couldn't see her. I heard her yell, "There's the water again!" I quickly looked at the pantry wall, and what I saw was water either leaving the wall, or bouncing off the wall.
>
> At this time there were twelve other adults in the five-room apartment. There were nine from the fire department, the landlord, Mr. Y-----, and his mother-in-law. This water squirting was happening in every room in the apartment.
>
> The police heard about it and came up. At one time while they were there, the daughter went into the pantry for a drink of water. One of the police officers followed her. When she turned and saw him she dropped the glass. The officer asked her if she had water in the glass, and she said no. I learned later that she did have water in the glass, but said no because she knew what

> the officer might think. After more questioning she admitted she did have water in the glass for a drink.
>
> Right then, the police decided that whatever damage had been done was done by the daughter. We knew this could not be true because, for one thing, she could not have got away with it with so many adults in the apartment, and further, it was also happening in Methuen at the same time.

The last paragraph is also important:

> Mrs. Y----- said that one time she had five relatives mopping up water in Methuen while the eleven-year-old was with her grandmother in Lawrence. The case had become so well known in Methuen that traffic jams were being caused by curious people. Strangers would go up to the Y-----s and touch their clothes with the thought that some spiritual help would be theirs. To avoid these problems, the Y-----s announced that a hole had been found in their roof which accounted for the water. The public believed this story, and the whole thing just died away. I contacted the Methuen Fire Department, and they told me why the Y-----s had made the statement. This still did not explain the situation in Lawrence.

I again wrote to the expert asking him if he thought that the girl could have possibly caused the water by a trick.

He replied that no trick had been used. "First, because it seems almost impossible for the girl to do that (tossing water about in large amounts) with so many people in the apartment, as I explained to you. Also, there is her grandmother's statement that water appeared in the living room before the girl got out of bed one morning."

I also contacted the Methuen Fire Department and received nothing but their official statement. It explained that water had been held in the insulation of the Y-----'s home. When enough water had collected, it was released inside the house. The water had come in by means of a hole in the roof.

In another letter the expert discussed this statement by the Methuen Fire Department:

> As for the Methuen Fire Department, they told me that they were giving out a story that they felt would end the curiosity. The story was a false one, of course. One of the big roofing companies was interested and they sent an inspector to Methuen for a few days. He came up with nothing as far as roof leaks or insulation, and the building was given a complete examination. As for the insulation, it could not possibly hold the water. It could get damp, or even wet, but when it did the water would flow downward and find its way out at the bottom. Further, if there had been a hole in the roof, the wetting or dampness would only be in the area of the hole, and not in all parts of the house.
>
> In the Lawrence case there was no insulation in the building, and as I have told you, the apartment is a second-floor apartment in a three-story building, and there was no dampness of any kind on the third floor.

I discussed the case also in letters with Reverend Guy J. Cyr, of the Sacred Heart Rectory in Lawrence, who had investigated the strange events. He had talked to the Y-----s and was very familiar with the entire affair. He did not believe that tricks had been used:

I am fully aware of the fact that there was an awful lot of water. One witness said that at one time he actually saw it running down the staircase. In one room, several people said, there was at least one inch of it on the floor. A few times, according to reports, as much as a quart of it would splash at once. There were many people there. Once there were as many as twenty-five.

Note here Mr. Y-----'s own words: "First, there is a noise like a firecracker, then the water shoots out."

I have to mention a few more facts reported by the witnesses: Just before each explosion a hissing noise was heard, lasting for about a second, just before the firecracker exploded. Then came the explosion, like the snapping of the thumb against one of the fingers, or like a firecracker. Then, or immediately after, the water was seen.

Rev. Cyr sent me another letter remarking that the officials in Methuen "gave a solution to the mystery knowing all the time that it was no solution at all, so that curious people would not bother Mr. and Mrs. Y----- any more."

In reviewing the case, it can be said that no normal explanations will do. The police report that the Y-----'s daughter finally admitted having water in a glass, does not, to my mind, change the main facts. The activities of the water poltergeist were seen by several witnesses. Again it must be remembered that the case is not the only example of the mysterious appearance of water, but is one of a number of its kind.

Recall

1. The mysterious appearance of water in Methuen was investigated by the Fire Department and (a) the eleven-year-old girl's science teacher (b) an expert from Harvard University (c) a representative of a roofing company.
2. When the girl went from Methuen to her grandmother's house in Lawrence, the water (a) stopped in Methuen and started in Lawrence (b) continued in Methuen and started in Lawrence (c) stopped altogether.
3. The Methuen Fire Department put out a false story on the mysterious water to (a) keep interest in the case alive (b) protect the Y-----s from curious people (c) cover up their own ignorance.
4. The Lawrence Police Department blamed the girl for the trouble when she (a) was seen by a police officer throwing water at a wall (b) confessed (c) admitted that she dropped a glass of water.
5. The author, Raymond Bayless, gives the events in the order in which (a) they happened (b) he learned of them (c) the police revealed them.

Infer

6. The events in Methuen show that (a) government officials do not always tell the truth (b) scientists can solve any problem they face (c) the eleven-year-old girl was responsible.

7. The Lawrence Police Department seemed most interested in (a) really solving the mystery (b) finding someone to blame (c) arresting the A-----s.
8. The story would probably be easier to believe if "the expert" who provided most of the information had (a) met any of the Y-----s or A-----s himself (b) been identified as a well-known scientist (c) not been so easily fooled by tricks.
9. The author probably included the letter from Reverend Cyr because (a) it offers many new facts (b) it differs greatly from other reports (c) the word of a priest would impress many readers.
10. The author's conclusion that "no normal explanations will do" seems (a) reasonable (b) too weak (c) prejudiced.

Vocabulary Review

1. Dad put *insulation* in my bedroom last fall. The insulation probably makes the room more (a) beautiful (b) comfortable (c) crowded.
2. Tommy put the leftover pie in the *pantry.* A *pantry* is a (a) refrigerator (b) kitchen (c) small storage room.
3. When our car was damaged, the insurance company sent a *representative* right away. A *representative* is a (a) check (b) letter (c) person.
4. Mom says she's so busy that the *spiritual* side of her life suffers. *Spiritual* refers to (a) religion (b) money (c) entertainment.
5. When Ms. Lichtenberger asked how the fight started, she got several *versions.* In other words, she got several (a) refusals (b) lies (c) stories.

Critical Thinking

1. What explanation did the Methuen Fire Department offer for the mysterious appearance of water? What facts seem to indicate that this explanation is not correct?

2. If you had been the Fire Chief in Methuen, would you have approved of the false story given to the public? Explain why, or why not.

3. What explanation did the Lawrence Police Department offer for the strange events? What facts seem to indicate that this explanation is not correct?

4. Do you believe that the strange events described in "Watery Poltergeists" really took place? Yes? No? Maybe? Explain the reasons for your opinion.